Shakespeare's Verse
a user's manual

by
ROGER GROSS

Shakespeare's Verse: A User's Manual for Actors, Directors, Readers, and Enlightened Teachers, Copyright 2015 by Roger Gross

All rights reserved. No part of this book may be reproduced or transmitted in any form or by any means, electronic or mechanical, including photocopying, recording, or by any information storage and retrieval system, without written permission from the author.

First edition
Printed in the United States of America
Book and cover design by Kelsey Rice

Library of Congress Catalog Number #2015940240
ISBN #978-1-942428-04-6

For Patricia
Forever

Praise for Shakespeare's Verse

"**The book is terrific.** *Shakespeare's Verse: A User's Manual* is an essential text for the actor and director; a comprehensive and persuasive method for tackling the challenge of speaking Shakespeare. Roger Gross' life-long love of Shakespeare is evident on every page as is his musician's ear. The result is an easy-to-understand, lively and most important, practical guide."

—MICHELE GALLERY, TWO-TIME EMMY AWARD WINNER

"**This book is a wonder!** Written in such a straightforward, almost conversational style, that no reader can possibly be inhibited by the material. It is delightfully short yet manages to be absolutely comprehensive."

— DR. ROBERT BARTON, AUTHOR OF THE POPULAR BOOK *ACTING: ONSTAGE AND OFF* AND SEVEN OTHERS

"Roger Gross brings his long history of directing Shakespeare both professionally and academically, as well as his years of scholarship, to his very readable, very practical guide to speaking Shakespeare's verse. It's **a treasure trove of information** and advice for lovers of Shakespeare at every level."

—DAKIN MATTHEWS, ACTOR, SCHOLAR AND PRODUCER

Also by Roger Gross:

Understanding Playscripts: Theory and Method

Shakespeare's Verse

*A USER'S MANUAL
for actors, directors, readers,
and enlightened teachers*

by
ROGER GROSS

www.ShakespearesVerse-UsersManual.com

Pen-L Publishing
Fayetteville, Arkansas
Pen-L.com

Acknowledgements

Anyone who has successfully completed the writing of a substantial book knows that the job isn't done alone. Writers depend on help of many kinds from many sources. I can't give proper thanks to all of those who helped me but I want, at least, to mention those who were most important to me during the near 40-year project.

The hundreds of students in my graduate and undergraduate "Acting Shakespeare" classes at the University of Arkansas, Bowling Green State University, Santa Clara University, and those students and professionals who acted in my productions, in their struggles and triumphs, taught me much.

Alene Bryson showed uncanny patience and diligence, doing computer textual analysis for me before we had computers. Kimberly Pennell and Patricia Gross became my other brains in the rush to the wire. I couldn't have done without them. Robert Barton gave the type script an invaluable last read.

I thank David Crystal and his son, Ben, for their extremely useful website, ShakespearesWords.com. The wonderful *Riverside Shakespeare* (Houghton Mifflin Company, Boston, 1974) is the source for my line citations.

I'll never be able to say enough about the value of being allowed to study at these great Shakespeare libraries: The Folger Shakespeare Library (Washington, D.C.); the Shakespeare Centre (Stratford on Avon); the British Museum Library (London); The Birmingham (England) Central Library. My deepest appreciation to the kind and generous staffs of these institutions.

Table of Contents

How This Happened xiii
   How Dare I Presume To Say All This? xviii
   To Be The Best, Work With The Best xix
The Problem 1
The Power of His Form 3
The Payoff 6
Shakespeare's Verse System 7
Shakespeare's Basic Verse Form 9
   His Not-Quite-Infinite Variety 13
   How He Varies The Stock Line 14
      The Feminine Ending 14
      The Inverted Foot 17
      The Cascade 23
      The Caesura 26
      The Silent Beat In Mid-Line 31
      The Shared Line 34
      Short Lines: A Shakespearean Code For Actors 36
      The Lilt 45
   There Are Exceptions: E.g. Accentual Verse 49
   And While We're At It, Another Syllabic Form 51
What Shapes The Way We Speak A Line? 55
Scansion One 56
   But There's a Catch 61
   And If You Don't? Massively Ruined Lines 70
Surprises That Complicate Scansion 72
   The Medial Vowel Elision: "Mid-V" 72
      Mid-V Exercises 74
   Some Words Have Variable Pronunciations 76
   Some Other Variable Words & Names 79
   The Last-Word Variation: "L-W Var" 80
      Examples: L-W Var in Close Proximity 87

  Compressions 88
  "Even," "E'en," and "E'vn" 90
  Words Ending in "Est" and " 'St" 94
  "Odd-Emps": Words with Unexpected Emphases 98
  "Heaven": A Great Place But a Hard Word (With Difficult Friends) 102
  Unfamiliar Word Pronunciations 105
  A Few Unfamiliar Name Pronunciations 108
  Unspoken Possessives 111
  "Many A" 114
  Invisible Contractions 116
  "Amer-Adds": Words to Which Americans Add an Unwanted Syllable 118
Scansion Two 120
  How Do You Stay Clear and Natural While Maintaining Verse Integrity? 120
  The Root of Good Acting 122
  Enemies of Shape And Color 124
  Modern Speech Quirks 125
    The "Not-Trap" 125
    The "Personal Pronoun-Trap" 127
  There Are No Quick Syllables in Blank Verse: The Diddley Menace 130
    Diddleys 131
    Diddley Work 133
    A Special Case of Diddleys: ". . . Able" 135
  Flowing and Chopping 140
  Unwanted Pauses 141
  Momentum Words at the Start of Lines 142
  Breathing and Pausing 146
    The Long-Line Challenge 146
  Vowel Shifts 149
    "O" and "Oh" 150
    Straight "U" Sounds 151
  Dialect 152
  Words; Figures of Speech; Rhetoric 153
  Antithesis: Shakespeare's Favorite Figure 155
  Imagery: How to Live in a Richer World 159

    His Developing Style 160
    Marking a Script 164
    Crucial Organic Strategy 168
Speeches for Scanning Practice With My Solutions 171

Appendix 1: End of The Beginning. So Now What? 179
Appendix 2: How I Did My Research and Why I Didn't Put That in the Book 181
Appendix 3: What About /uu/ and /--/? Why No /—uu/? Why No /--u/ 183
Appendix 4: How to Get Help Pronouncing Shakespeare's Words 185
Appendix 5: The Conversation 187

Shakespeare wrote
the world's greatest verse plays.
Almost all of them are performed
or read as prose, by default,
not by decision.
This is a tragic waste, but it is fixable.

This book has two goals:
- to persuade you that the great rewards of verse speaking and reading are worth much more than the modest effort required to master them.
- to provide the information and guidance needed to lead you down this path.

HOW THIS HAPPENED

Many years ago, I was the Artistic Director of the California Shakespeare Festival, an Actors' Equity company and a very good one. At our peak, many people told us we were the best acting ensemble in the country.

I believed it and there was good reason for it. When James Dunn and I founded the Festival, we had a dream and a plan. The dream was for a kind of vigorous, earthy, deeply humanistic Shakespeare. The plan was to hire the best actors we could find, to keep them together year after year, and to train them as well as to use them. The company included such fine actors as David Ogden Stiers (who, at that time, could play any male role in the canon), Kurtwood Smith, Dakin Matthews, David Dukes, Elizabeth Huddle, Carolyn Reed-Dunn, Joan Schirle and many others of great skill.

It was a wonderful dream and an effective plan. Within a few years, it produced shows of power and delight. We pleased our audiences and ourselves. We even pleased the professors of English . . . almost. But there was, too often, a qualification in their praise: "Wonderful, exciting . . . of course you massacred the verse . . . but it was great nevertheless."

I reveled in the praise and brushed off the quibble about the verse because, frankly, I didn't know what they were talking about. I thought we spoke the text very well. I now blush at the naiveté of my response.

After eight years of playing the dual role of professional director and full-time college professor, I had to make a choice. The Festival at this time was running two theatres for five months a year and needed to lengthen its season yet again. The time for riding two horses at once was over. I decided that my heart lay more with the academic theatre.

I brought a lot of things with me from the Festival. Above all, the nagging question, "What the hell do they mean 'we massacred the verse?'" I decided to find an answer to the question. It should be easy, I thought. I'll study a couple of the best books on speaking the verse and resolve that question.

What a shock to find that there were no such books. There were shelves of books about Shakespeare's poetry, that is, his metaphors and figures of speech and his other ways with language, but none of any value about performing his verse.

In my disappointment and eagerness, I did the obvious thing; I hurried to the professors who had complained so.

THE PROF

Well . . . you see . . . um . . . it's written in . . . uh . . . blank verse and . . . er . . . you need to speak it . . . that way.

ROGER

Yes, of course, I know it's blank verse. But what do you mean . . . "speak it that way?"

THE PROF

Well . . . you know . . . speak it as verse . . . blank verse.

ROGER

But more exactly . . . what were we not doing?

THE PROF

Well . . . um . . . the rhythm.

ROGER

Yes, what about it?

THE PROF

You've got to get it right.

ROGER

Could you be more specific?

THE PROF

Alright . . . it has to be like . . . blank verse rhythm.

ROGER
Which is?

THE PROF
You know: dee DUM, dee DUM, dee DUM, dee DUM, dee DUM.

ROGER
That's it? You don't mean that literally, do you? That every line should be spoken in that deadly humdrum beat? Actually many of the lines don't seem to fit that beat. Most of them have too many syllables and many of them seem to want emphasis in the wrong place. But mainly it just sounds boring: always a light emphasis followed by a heavy emphasis.

THE PROF
Well, it **is** iambic pentameter, and we should respect the playwright.

I admit that this is a bit of a parody of my conversations with many teachers. I expected them to know about the verse, these teachers of poetry and of Shakespeare. But the gist of it is true. In fact, when I listen to professors of Shakespeare and other poetry specialists reading Shakespeare aloud, I never hear them read him as verse. They sense, vaguely, that the productions they see are not done as verse, but they don't, in fact, know exactly what that means or how to speak verse themselves, with the exception of a precious few who are blessed with an intuitive grasp of verse rhythm.

I found, to my amazement, that skill in speaking verse was a lost art. In the nineteenth century, the scholars got interested in other aspects of poetry and lost track of some of the most fundamental facts and strategies of verse form.

This apparent dead end whetted my desire to know. Something convinced me that there was a lost treasure and it was findable. Turned out I was right. But rather than in the modern scholarship, I found my most useful study to be of the sources from approximately 100 years before to 100 years after Shakespeare's birth.

I've been working on this research project and testing the results in production for forty years. I came across a precious pair of 19th century scholars who looked carefully at parts of the territory which had been so completely ignored by the others: William Sidney Walker (*A Critical Examination of the Text of Shakespeare, c. 1854*) and E.A. Abbot (*A Shakespearian Grammar, c. 1901*). Much of value appeared in Helge Kokeritz's work (*Shakespeare's Pronunciation*, 1953).

As I searched, a few other scholars began working similar ground. For years I had the advantage of being the only researcher who was also a theatre person, able to fully test my work pragmatically.

Finally, in the last ten years, an awareness of the need has developed and a few accomplished theatre artists have spread the gospel. Paul Meier, an outstanding director and scholar, and Dakin Matthews, a fine actor, have published good, useful books to fuel the fire. Two of the great professional theatre artists, Peter Hall and Barry Edelstein, stepped forward to write strongly and soundly in support of the verse. Meanwhile, academic critics such as George T. Wright and Marina Tarlinskaja produced impressive works of scholarship which, however, did not deal with the issue of performance. Other academic critics did work so esoteric that they seemed unrelated to our topic.

A few others have very recently written chapters on "scansion" but most of these suffer from fundamental flaws and are based more on tradition than on research. They do not go deeply enough into the subject to serve the actor or student who wants thorough instruction in "how to do it." Somewhere in between lies Adrian Noble's useful "How to Do Shakespeare."

My special contribution has been to take what we have learned about the rhythms further, to explore the implications for performance. And I have found several patterns, Shakespearean habits, previously overlooked.

My research questions were:

- what was Shakespeare's verse form and strategy and what does it demand of us as actors, as speakers, and readers of his verse?
- what insights does verse form give to the meanings of the play, the life of our characters, and the demands and opportunities for staging?

The answers to these questions were much richer than expected and I'm here to share them with you for your profit and delight in what I believe is the first practical manual for Shakespearean verse speech and reading.

You may wonder why I keep referring to "verse reading." In case it's not obvious, I had better point out that everything you'll learn here about what makes Shakespeare's text verse rather than prose applies equally to acting and to silent reading. Verse rhythm yields its benefits wherever it is felt. Silent reading without an appropriate rhythm is as impoverished as prose acting of verse text.

HOW DARE I PRESUME TO SAY ALL THIS?

In my search, working in the world's greatest Shakespeare libraries, I explored the relevant prosodic and pronunciation evidence from 1450 till now, not just from versification sources but from a wide range of related territories. I did metrical analyses of not only Shakespeare but of other playwrights and poets, good and bad, from at least a hundred years before and after him. Amazing things of great value to actors and directors appeared.

None of this is merely my bright idea. This approach has been tested again and again in both the classroom and in most of the forty Shakespearean productions I have directed and the many more that I have produced or coached. Because this is a practical handbook, meant to be used by actors, directors, students and devotees "in the heat of battle" as you might say, I have not burdened it with the citations of the research that led me to these conclusions. What I have learned from experience, however, is that those who learn to speak according to the guidelines given here invariably sense the rightness and need no further persuasion. You can trust it.

This handbook is a practical user's manual based on what I learned. If you master what is here, your performances of Shakespeare will be richer and more powerful.

My greatest dream is that you will master these techniques, embrace the dream of Shakespeare played as verse, and will go forth to teach others to do likewise.

> "Speak the speech, I pray you, as I pronounced it to you, trippingly on the tongue. But if you mouth it, as many of our players do, I had as lief the town-crier spoke my lines."
> –The Man Himself

TO BE THE BEST, WORK WITH THE BEST

It is a common belief that Shakespeare is the greatest writer in history. He is surely the most popular playwright. He was then; he is now. His plays are done all over the world. You wouldn't want to have to count the number of productions of Shakespeare each year. It is astonishing for a four-hundred-plus-year-old writer . . . for any writer of any time, any place.

In the first half of 2012, over twenty-five films were made based on Shakespeare scripts. No one else comes near. In 2000, the English voted him "Man of the Millennium." Not Playwright of the Millennium . . . Man of the Millennium. You can't watch a night of television without hearing some reference to Shakespeare, and not just in drama or in high-toned programs; he's in the commercials. Why? Because he's memorable. Because he said it better. It's hard to speak our language without quoting him.

In the acting trade, Shakespeare's scripts are considered the best of all training grounds. If you can master the problems of Shakespearean acting, you can handle anything. He used more of the possible playwriting tools than anyone and therefore requires that actors have more tools. He provides a greater challenge and, therefore, a greater opportunity.

> **TESTIMONY OF THE SKILLED & FAMOUS**
>
> "There is no better way for an actor to train his intellect, his body, his breathing, his voice and his skills in communicating with an audience than by playing Shakespeare. It is an Olympic course in acting."
>
> So says Peter Hall, founder of the Royal Shakespeare Company, long-time director of the Royal National Theatre of England, one of the best.

Shakespeare is like acting any other playwright. Yet there are crucial differences and until you master these special techniques, you'll never get to the heart of Shakespeare.

The most important difference is the speaking of the verse.

The actor's/reader/s job is to give us a line—so strongly charged that the audience can't help but follow the structure of meaning and feeling as Shakespeare imagined it.

THE PROBLEM

Most of what Shakespeare wrote, he wrote in verse. The problem is that almost all of us speak the plays as prose, not by choice but for lack of sufficient knowledge of the form. Speaking good verse as if it were prose is like performing a good song without the music.

This verse has the power to enhance the strength and clarity of Shakespeare's plays tremendously **with no loss of naturalness or spontaneity.** When it is spoken well, it affects the audience deeply without them being consciously aware that they are hearing verse.

To speak it well, you need only understand the simple rules of the form, apply them to each of your verse lines, and learn a few quirks of Shakespeare's pronunciation.

> **If you discover the correct rhythm for each line before you learn it, the rhythmic shape will become part of what you mean by the line, how you feel about it.**
> **It will become the music you need to express yourself. This will protect your spontaneity and keep you from sounding pedantic or mechanical.**

Shakespeare knew what he was doing. He made his music match his meanings. When you get the music right, it's hard to get the meaning wrong. Though the rules of the form are pretty strict, they aren't confining. There is still plenty of room for expression of the actor's and the character's individuality.

I want to repeat two of those sentences because they deal with the concern some actors have when they are asked to learn the verse system, the fear that they must choose between being correct and being natural:

> **. . . verse has the power to enhance the strength and clarity of Shakespeare's plays tremendously with no loss of naturalness or spontaneity. When it is spoken well, it affects the audience very deeply without them being consciously aware that they are hearing verse.**

THE POWER OF HIS FORM

We aren't used to writers who have complete mastery of their form. Most writers are able to find only approximate means of communicating their vision. With such scripts, directors and actors grab a rough idea of character and action from the text and then follow their own imagination to invent a form that is mostly their own. For those of you who like technical terms, we say these writers suggest only a few **Parameters** and provide very loose **Limits of Tolerance** . . . like a cheap car. If there is little precision in the playwright's form, there will be a lot of latitude for free invention in the work of the actor and director and the limits of this invention are only vaguely drawn by the scripts.

With a fine sports car, you pay for the precision and you have to know plenty to get the best of it. Same with a fine play.

You have probably noticed that Shakespeare's scripts contain very few stage directions, probably fewer than you think since most of the directions in the modern editions were added by editors long after Shakespeare was gone.

Don't let the lack of stage directions fool you. It doesn't mean, "Whoopee! We're free to do whatever we want!"

> **Shakespeare gives an actor more precise information about how the play is to be performed than any other writer. That information is embedded in the verse form and in other poetic qualities of his text. It is implied by the verse rhythms and the textures of the verse. Information on speed, character, and every aspect of performance is waiting for the actor who is smart enough and ambitious enough to learn the language of dramatic verse. His Parameters are many and demanding and his Limits of Tolerance are tight and rigorous. Like that fine sports car.**

At which point, I think I hear several sighs from the back of the room, maybe a mutter of "old fogey," perhaps an outright confrontation from one of the bold ones: "Oh, man, there have been hundreds of far-out productions of *Hamlet*, no two alike, very interesting. Now you want us to make 'em all alike? Boring!" To which I, sighing right back, say: "Yes, there have been several hundred honorable *Hamlet*s, some brilliant and radically unlike what had gone before. What they had in common was that each fulfilled the **Parameters** of the script (i.e. was what the script implied a *Hamlet* needed to be) and each found its unique creative world, its unique portion of the **Latitude**, within the **Limits of Tolerance** implied by the script."

Meanwhile, for every one of these, about ten others (some "far out" and some "traditional") missed the boat, failed to be honorable productions of *Hamlet* because they didn't fulfill those Parameters and/or lived outside the range of Tolerance implied by the script.

THE THREE BASIC KINDS OF PARAMETER
LAID DOWN BY A SHAKESPEAREAN SCRIPT ARE:
1. ACTION,
2. CHARACTER
3. VERSE RHYTHM

THE PATH TO ACTION AND CHARACTER IS VERSE.

Shakespeare's scripts are meticulously, thoughtfully, crafted. His craft yields a commanding form that may be disobeyed only at great cost. At first glance, you may see nothing. The more you study, the more you will see.

And this will go on forever.

> **Verse is not a straitjacket. Verse is not a stifling limiter of your creativity. Verse is the firm foundation on which creative acts may be performed. This is the great liberator of Shakespeare's power, the key to his Inner Sanctum.**

Once you have this foundation, this guidance system, in place, you will have the freedom to explore and invent, with the confidence that what you create will serve the text as the text serves you.

Learning to speak the verse is not a matter of academic propriety. It's not about cultural prestige or any other trivial motive. It is the secret of great Shakespearean acting. Master it and you will be miles ahead of the competition.

THE PAYOFF

If you make the smart choice, if you decide to invest the little time it takes to learn Shakespeare's way of doing things, you not only get the amazing bounty of interpretive help I describe above, but also the essential information which allows you to be Shakespeare's collaborator rather than his competitor or impediment. And you also get, for the same price, several other great benefits. (I know . . . I'm beginning to sound like a late-night TV pitchman. But it's true.)

About twenty of my Shakespeare productions were done after I learned the secrets of the verse. I was a pretty good director before I understood the verse and I built some very good productions which audiences liked a lot. I specialized in energy and athleticism, in fast, non-stop activity. I now blush to say that our slogan at the California Shakespeare Festival was "Blood and Guts Shakespeare." We wanted people to know it wouldn't be boring.

So the shows were good. But in some very important ways, they were better after I learned to teach actors to speak the verse. Here are the most important differences between verse productions and what you're used to hearing.
If you speak verse:

- Your speech will be clearer.
- The play will move much faster.
- You will be more fully energized.
- The verse will exert a subliminal control of the audience making the play more effective and affective through interplay of the underlying meter and the immediate rhythm.
- The unity of melody and meaning will amplify all meanings and emotions.
- Clues to meaning will emerge.

SHAKESPEARE'S VERSE SYSTEM

> ### THE BEAT AND THE LINE: HERE IS THE HEART OF IT
>
> Verse is primarily a matter of RHYTHM.
> Rhythm is a matter of the number of BEATS,
> the length of the LINE,
> and the pattern of EMPHASIS.
> The exhilaration and power of verse are rooted in the driving force of THE BEAT, in the security of its predictability, and in the titillation and emphasis which come from the unexpected thwarting of our expectations by RHYTHMIC VARIATIONS.
> The regularity of the BEAT and the steady pattern of EMPHASIS make us feel we know what to expect. They make speech feel "right"; they make the words, the ideas, seem inevitable and irresistible, no matter how unexpected.

The audience has to feel the beat to hear the music.

If you like strong-beat music, particularly if you like to dance to it, you know how important that **sense of the beat** is. You may not even know what a one-beat is but you will find the music undanceable if you don't **feel** the one-beat clearly.

**We only ride a rhythm when we feel
where the rhythmic units begin and end.**

In Shakespeare's verse, the rhythmic unit is the line.

In music we need to feel the start of the phrase and the start of each bar. In verse, the end of each line and the start of the next are the crucial "locaters" that allow the audience to feel the beat, to savor it, to draw meaning from it. No matter how complicated Shakespeare's "variations" get, the actor must find a way to make the shape of the underlying rhythm clear.

Reveal the shape of the line.
Drive the beat.

SHAKESPEARE'S BASIC VERSE FORM

Once Shakespeare has caught us in the spell of his basic beat, he can toy with our expectations, twisting and turning, creating swoops and leaps which are musically thrilling in themselves and which also clarify his meanings and channel our attention. But first we need to understand **the basic Line and Beat.**

Shakespeare's most common rhythm is called
IAMBIC PENTAMETER.

> **Iambic pentameter
> is a verse line of five iambic feet.**
>
> **An iamb is a verse foot
> made up of two syllables,
> the first syllable relatively lighter
> than the second.**

Burn this definition into your memory. It is absolutely fundamental. You need to go far beyond "knowing about" it. You need to become so familiar with this Beat that you spontaneously feel any violation of it, that you feel its power and learn to exploit it, learn to use it as the engine which drives your speech.

Shakespeare's Basic Verse Form

Unrhymed Iambic Pentameter is called **BLANK VERSE.**

> **You may have heard a different definition of the iambic pentameter line: "a verse line with five light emphases and five heavy emphases, alternating." This is flat-out wrong. "Light" and "heavy" have meaning only relatively and only within each foot.**
>
> **If anyone asks you "how many heavy beats in an iambic pentameter line?" tell them the question is nonsense. The iambic pentameter form tells us nothing about how many (absolutely) heavy or light beats there should be. A perfect iambic pentameter line may be made of ten heavy syllables or ten light syllables or five of each or almost any combination.**
>
> **What the iambic pentameter form tells us is there will be five iambic feet and that each of those feet will have a relatively light syllable followed by a relatively heavier syllable.**

It is possible for the relatively light beat in one foot to be heavier than the relatively heavy beat in the previous foot. A relatively emphatic syllable isn't necessarily "punched." A relatively light syllable may be "punched" very hard. **Meaning, character, and situation** determine the degree of emphasis. The verse form says only that the relatively emphatic syllable should be **somewhat** more emphatic than the relatively light syllable.

Let's arbitrarily say that there are ten possible degrees of emphasis; 1 indicates the lightest emphasis and 10 indicates the heaviest. The wrong definition of iambic pentameter implies that every line would have to alternate between an emphasis from 1 to 5 and an emphasis from 6 to 10. Down up, down up, down up . . . *et cetera*. Something like this:

1, 6 / 2, 6 / 3, 9 / 5, 10 / 3, 8

In this example, / 1, 6 / is an iambic foot, as is each pair that follows. The slashes indicate the division between feet. Get used to these markings.

If we spoke this way, we would be extremely artificial and boring.
Here is an example of a possible, correct iambic pentameter line according to the proper definition:
    1, 2 / 1, 2 / 1, 2 / 1, 2 / 1, 2 (very light)

So is this:
    9, 10 / 9, 10 / 9, 10 / 9, 10 / 9, 10   (extraordinarily heavy)

These aren't very interesting lines but they are correct.

This, too, is a correct iambic pentameter line:
    1, 2 / 3, 4 / 5, 6 / 7, 8 / 9, 10

(which is also an extreme example of a Shakespeare favorite, "the Cascade," which we will consider soon).

And this: 9, 10 / 7, 8 / 5, 6 / 3, 4 / 1, 2

You see that the iambic demand can be satisfied in many ways.

The only rule is that the second syllable in a foot should be relatively more emphatic than the first.

A common way of indicating an iamb is: **u –**
("**u**" = relatively lighter; "**–**" = relatively heavier)

This is a common way of indicating an iambic pentameter line:
    u – / u – / u – / u – / u –

This is a **STOCK LINE** (five feet, ten syllables, strictly iambic) and therefore it ends on a relatively emphatic syllable. Such a line is said to have a **MASCULINE ENDING**. (Don't blame me for that.)

TESTIMONY FROM THE SKILLED AND FAMOUS:

"The return of the voice also enabled me to begin really to taste the verse. I discovered that it was like surfing. Unlike most modern writing, the words, the metre and rhythm contain their own energy. Once you've liberated it, it carries you forward effortlessly. It's a question of putting one's brain into the words and one's emotion into the rhythm. The metaphors have such a vigorous life of their own that they sweep through one unaided; that is to say, if the rhythmic conduit has been firmly established."

Simon Callow, one of Britain's best actors and directors, from his book, *Being an Actor*

"Once you've liberated it, it carries you forward . . ."

Believe it!

HIS NOT-QUITE-INFINITE VARIETY

Shakespeare's verse is not absolutely strict. He was master of the **strategic variation**. Perfectly strict verse is boring. If you want to see how inventive Shakespeare is, just read the verse of his stricter amateur contemporaries. If you want to see how brilliantly he controlled his variations from strict form, read his freer professional contemporaries, whose verse often is so uncontrolled that it seems to be prose.

> **Shakespeare had a dramatic purpose in every choice he made. Your job is to find a subtextual purpose that makes sense of each choice in the context of your character, the scene, and the play as a whole. When you face up to this challenge, you make one of your most profound creative contributions to the play.**

No playwright has more successfully used the possibilities of a strong basic beat and the full range of variations within it.

Our job is to discover and understand this potent music so that we can recreate it in our speech.

HOW HE VARIES THE STOCK LINE

Shakespeare allowed himself a limited number of **strategic variations** on the basic form; devices that thwart expectations and vitalize the stock line. With these few variations, he forged verse of subtlety, delicacy, eloquence, and power beyond what any other playwright has achieved.

Pay special attention to these variations. Once you have mastered the basic form, you'll find that **the real excitement is in playing these variations against the driving master beat**.

Here are his favorite ways of surprising expectations, imaging feelings, enhancing texture, and directing attention: Feminine Ending, Inverted Foot, Short Lines, 6- and 6½-foot Lines, Last-word Variations, Caesura, and Silent Beat in Mid-line.

THE FEMININE ENDING

This is Shakespeare's most common variation. In about 18% of his verse lines, Shakespeare uses eleven syllables, adding a relatively unemphatic syllable to the end of a line. **This beat requires a brief pause at the end of the line**, even when the sense of the sentence flows on into the next line without punctuation. This pause is slightly longer than the lilt-suspension of a ten-syllable line. (See page 45.)

If you run through a feminine ending into the next line, the beat evaporates. Don't do it!

Marina Tarlilnskaja counted them all and found that they fall into four periods as Shakespeare's style developed. In his early period, 10.8 % of his lines had feminine endings. In the next, he used 18.4%, then, 26.09%, and finally a surprising 32.9% of his lines ended with an eleventh, relatively light syllable. Clearly, he found this variation more useful and so should we.

The feminine ending breaks the regularity of the rhythm in useful ways and focuses a little extra attention on the word which begins the next line. Even more important, the pause allows the audience to keep track of the basic beat, to feel the shape of the line.

Here is an example of a **feminine ending:**

   1, 2 / 1, 3 / 1, 2 / 1, 4 / 1,   2 / 1
   To **be**, or **not** to **be**–that **is** the **ques**-tion: HAM 3.1.56

I scanned this on a four-point scale; that is, as if there were only four levels of emphasis. But many degrees of emphasis are possible; more than we have patience to indicate or need to discuss, but not more than a subtle actor uses routinely.

In the four-point system**, 1 = the lightest** of four degrees of emphasis; **4 = the heaviest**. A "slash mark" (/) **indicates the end of one foot and beginning of another**.

Don't worry; actors aren't expected to put numbers on their lines like this. Once the verse demands of the line are understood, rationalized in the form of subtext, and "absorbed," the actor's intuition, sense of purpose, and attitude will generate the nuances of emphasis. We only use the numbers when we want to describe the shape of a line in writing.

Did I make that sound easy enough: "Once the verse demands of the line are understood, rationalized in the form of subtext, and absorbed?" Well, it's not easy. This is some of the interpreter's hardest creative work. The feminine ending has no firm meaning. Everything depends on the context.

Look at the early scenes in *The Winter's Tale*: King Leontes, in a fit of jealousy, rants. In a first 19-line unit, 42% of the lines are feminine. In the 2nd, 22-line unit, it's 36%, and in the third, 13-line unit, we find an amazing 61% have that eleventh syllable.

Are you tempted to think that the feminine ending is obviously Shakespeare's way of showing an overwrought mind? Well, take a look at the disturbed mind of Mercutio in *Romeo and Juliet's* Queen Mab speech: 49 lines without a single feminine ending. **The question you must deal with is "What thought or feeling would cause me to hesitate briefly at a relatively less emphatic moment? Why do I need to do it and how can I use it?**

There is one generalization I feel safe making: a cluster of feminine endings means a significant change in the scene. Hunt it down.

DID SHAKESPEARE REALLY CARE ABOUT THIS VERSE STUFF?

CELIA:
Didst thou hear these verses?

ROSALIND:
O, yes, I heard them all, and more too, for some of them had in them more feet than the verses would bear.

CELIA:
That's no matter: the feet might bear the verses.

ROSALIND:
Ay, but the feet were lame, and could not bear themselves without the verse, and therefore stood lamely in the verse.

AYL.3.2.159-166

WELL, I GUESS SO!

THE INVERTED FOOT

The second most common variation is the INVERTED FOOT. An inverted iamb is the opposite of a stock iamb: a relatively heavy syllable is followed by a relatively light one. This is one of Shakespeare's most powerful devices.

What is most interesting about an inverted foot is that, when bonded with the iamb following, it creates a four syllable unit that I call a **"Swoop"** which gives a very special lift to a line. I'm convinced that this is the way Shakespeare thought of it because this is the way it plays most effectively. Think of an inversion not as one reversed foot but as **a four syllable moment** which starts high, plunges down to the depths, and **Swoops** back up to the heights again. It should feel like that moment when a roller coaster reaches the peak of a rise, Swoops down, and flies back up to the next peak.

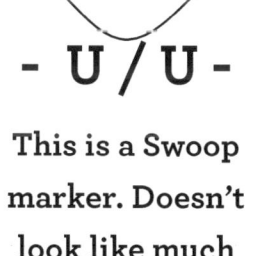

This is a Swoop marker. Doesn't look like much but it stands for a lot of power.

Don't minimize the energy of a Swoop.
Play it strongly. It has been put there to seize attention and energize. Make it so.

In case anyone asks you, an inverted iamb has its own name. It is called a trochee.
(TROH-kee)

Shakespeare's inversions are very cleverly placed to reveal the twists and turns of thought and feeling.

They only do their work when the actor <u>discovers</u> their purposes.

Inversions of the first foot:

These are the most common. About 14% of the lines have this inversion.
Here is an example:

```
   -   u /  u    -  / u   - / u   -  / u   -
 Vill–ain, thou knowst no law of God nor man                R3 1.2.70
```

Inversions of the fourth foot:

These are next most common at approximately 3%.
Here is an example:

```
   u   - / u   -    / u  - /  -   u / u   -  / u
 Which ren -ders good  for bad, bless-ings for cur - ses.
 (note the feminine ending)                                 R3 1.2.69
```

Inversions of the third foot:

These are the next most common at roughly 2%.
Here is an example:

```
   u    - / u     - / -   u / u   - / u   -
 As – sure your - self, af - ter our ship did split         TN 1.3.9
```

Here is an extraordinary example from *Romeo and Juliet* in which Romeo has three third-foot inversions in a row. I hope you can see what special excitement this rhetorical trick creates. ("being" = 1 syllable)

Love is a smoke <u>rais'd with</u> the fume of sighs;	ROM 1.1.190
Being purg'd, a fire <u>sparkling</u> in lovers' eyes;	ROM 1.1.191
Being vex'd, a sea <u>nourish'd</u> with lovers' tears.	ROM 1.1.192

Inversions of the first and third feet in one line:

These are next at about 1%.
Here is an example:

      —   u / u — / — u / u — / u —
      Hav - ing his ear full of his air - y fame,   TC 1.3.144

Inversions of the first and third feet have enormous energy.

Inversions of the first and fourth feet are rare.

      — u / u   — / u   — / — u / u   —
      Wound it   with sigh -ing, girl, kill it   with groans,   TIT 3.2.15

Inversions of the second foot are rare.

Inversions of the fifth foot do not occur.

MORE LINES WITH INVERSIONS

Each of these lines is stock except for the variation it illustrates.

1st foot inversion:

      —   u / u — / u   —   / u   — / u —

Check'ring the eastern clouds with streaks of light,	ROM 2.2.189
Many for many virtues excellent,	ROM 2.3.9
Virtue itself turns vice being misapplied, (being=1 syll.)	ROM 2.3.17
Need and oppression starveth in thy eyes,	ROM 5.1.70

4th foot inversion:

```
u  -  / u  -  / u  - / -  u / u  -
```
O, then dear saint, let lips do what hands do!   ROM 1.5.103
For I am falser than vows made in wine.   AYL 3.5.73
Met we on hill, in dale, forest or mead,   MND 2.1.83

3rd foot inversion:

```
u  -  / u   -  / -   u / u  - / u  -
```
As Nep- tune's park, rib - bed and pal - ed in   CYM 3.1.20
Tri-um- phant - ly tread on thy coun - try's ruin   COR 5.3.116

1st and 3rd feet inverted in one line:

```
-   u / u   - / -   u / u  - / u  -
```
That you know well. Some thing it is I would –   ANT 1.3.89
Wings and no eyes fig - ure un-hee- dy haste.   MND 1.1.237

1st and 4th feet inverted in one line:

```
-    u / u  -  / u   - / -   u / u   -
```
Ears with out hands or eyes, smell - ing sans all.   HAM 3.4.80
Li - ons more con - fi - dent, moun-tains and rocks   KJ 2.1.452
Wound it with sigh - ing, girl, kill it with groans,   TIT 3.2.15

2nd foot inversion: *Very* rare. **5th foot inversion** *never* **happens.**

> Inversions are never accidental.
> They are never unimportant.
> Search for inversions in your script.
> Play with them.
> Explore them.

> Play with these lines. Find more like them. Look for the rhythmic effect of the inversions. See what kind of meanings and feelings you can express by using them.

Here is an example of a line which demonstrates both an inversion and the relativity of emphasis. It is scanned on an eight-point scale (1 = lightest; 8 = heaviest):

```
  6   3 / 2   7 / 2    4 / 5   6 / 7    8
Rum-ble thy bel – ly – ful! Spit fire! Spout rain!                KL 3.2.14
```

Of course this is not the only reasonable way to speak the line.

Note that the last 3 feet = a Cascade. It is possible for the "heavy" syllable of one foot to be lighter than the "light" syllable of the following foot. In fact, this is a most common occurrence in Shakespeare. These Cascades, straight builds of two or three feet, are sprinkled throughout the verse.

Actors often come to me early in the rehearsal period to express frustration over their desire to emphasize a syllable which they think the verse form won't allow because it is a "light" syllable. Almost always, my answer is "go ahead; emphasize it. Just be sure you emphasize the next syllable a little bit more."

> **The light/heavy rule is relative only to single feet.**
> I don't want to drive you crazy by repeating this but it is a crucial idea and one which is too easy to forget.

> **1ST POP QUIZ:**
> ME: How many heavy beats in a blank verse line?
> YOU: Can't fool me with that one. Could be any # from 1 to 10. Depends on the meaning and mood of the scene. It's all relative.
> ME: An A for U!

THE CASCADE

One of Shakespeare's most common devices for keeping his iambic form regular without overusing the up and down pattern is a structure I call "the **Cascade**." It also allows him to give meaningful emphasis to relatively less emphatic syllables.

The **Cascade** is a sequence of two or more iambic feet with constantly rising emphasis. In a Cascade, each foot is correctly iambic but also, in each foot, the relatively lighter syllable is actually more emphatic than the relatively more emphatic syllable in the previous foot. OK, stop and think about it for a moment.

For example: 1, 2 / 3, 6 / 7, 9 / 3, 4 / 3, 5

The first three feet in this example are a **Cascade**. Each syllable is somewhat more emphatic than the syllable that precedes it. You'll find many lines of this kind in Shakespeare.

Here is an example: (We indicate a cascade by drawing a constantly rising line from its first to last syllables. Slashes indicate the beginning and end of a verse line.)

    That my woe-wearied tongue is still and mute.   R3 4.4.18

This is a two-foot Cascade. Our first inclination is probably to lose the iambic form and emphasize "woe" more than "wear . . . ", perhaps to scan it

    u u – / u u –
    That my woe wear-ied tongue

which is **anapestic**, not iambic. That is not Shakespeare's way. What the Cascade allows you to do is emphasize "woe," which is, no doubt, an important word, and then top it with "wearied," which is even more important.

Here is another two-foot Cascade:

> _____
> And the beholders of this frantic play,   R3 4.4.68

This would be a very awkward line without the Cascade. We generally find it difficult to deal with "the," "and," "an," "but," "in," "for" and such words when they fall in the relatively emphatic position in a foot. Shakespeare often asks us to do this. The Cascade is the solution. Without it, the line sounds very clumsy. The Cascade not only solves such problems; it also energizes a line. The constantly rising emphasis lifts us very effectively.

And here is a rare double-cascade line:

> _____ _____
> When to the sessions of sweet silent thought   SONN 30.1

The temptation here is to slip into dactylic verse; — u u / — u u / — u u / u. The Cascade will save you from sounding silly.

Here are two more two-footers:

> _____
> As an unperfect actor on the stage   SONN 23.1

With the SONN 23 example, Modern Speech Quirks tempt us to drop "as an" and to give "un" a big kick in the pants, subverting the iambic form. But Cascade the first 4 syllables and all's well.

> _____
> Will you go sister? Shepherd, ply her hard.   AYL 3.5.76

This one is hopeless without the Cascade. A speaker who drops "go" below "you," gives a very misleading cue; that dropped "go" is a standard cue for an alternate meaning of "go" which is not appropriate here (the "go" in "go figure" or "go crazy"). This is another line that will tempt us to lose our iambic form. We'll be inclined to speak it / 2, 2 / 8, 3 / 3 (Will you **go** sister?) With "Will you" and "sister" spoken as quick syllables. **But there are no quick syllables in Shakespeare. There are quick tempos, but no quick syllables.**

... when you speak a line in correct iambic form and it sounds "clunky," when it seems to ask you to emphasize less important words more than the really important ones, the first remedy to try is the Cascade. It is one of Shakespeare's most common devices.

THE CAESURA

Look at this lovely line:

> 'Tis not so sweet now as it was before.   TN 1.1.8

That's as regular as it gets: a perfect iambic pentameter stock line, no complicated syntax, all but one word has only one syllable and that one has only two. No variations here. Sweet simplicity.

Try speaking the line; see how easily it slips off your tongue. Don't let the relatively strong emphasis of "as" throw you. Give it full value. Don't give in to the modern-quirk temptation to punch "now."

Let's try something just a little more complex:

> Why, so I do, the noblest that I have.   TN 1.1.17

In several ways, it is as simple as the first line: perfectly iambic, one-syllable words. But that comma in the middle of the line means that we have moved into the world of **the Caesura.**

Traditionally, the **Caesura** has been defined as a **pause** mid-line. That is simplistic. Here is a somewhat better description:

A Caesura is a hesitation near the middle of a verse line.

It is not accidental, cosmetic or merely convenient.

It is organically functional and must be earned subtextually.

What **is** true is that something new happens at the **Caesura**. Dramatically and linguistically. The tide changes in some way. It may be small or it may be huge, but something changes.

For our purposes, it is most useful to divide Caesuras into two groups: the Major and the Minor, based on their impact on the line and their dramatic power. The dividing line is the point at which it becomes necessary to call the Caesura a **Variation**. The **Minor Caesura** is not disruptive of the Stock Line enough to be called a Variation. The **Major Caesura** is.

A comma in mid-line usually but not always is the sign of a **Minor Caesura**. The **Major Caesura** is usually indicated by the marks that call for more or less emphatic stops; marks like the colon, the semi-colon, the dash, the period, the exclamation mark and the question mark.

The line immediately above (TN 1.1.17) has what I would call a fairly significant Minor Caesura. Ignore the first comma; it's one of those misbegotten editors' additions which encourage pauses where they don't belong. It does not appear in the *First Folio*. (See the section on "Momentum Words.") The second comma, however, separates two phrases of very different function and flavor. It is a Caesura and an effective one because it mimics the twist in Orsino's word play, (hart/heart). "Why, so I do," provokes puzzlement and curiosity in this context and "the noblest that I have" springs a "heart/hart" pun and probably unleashes a bit of disappointment among the courtiers who have had almost enough of suffering for love and are ready to go hunting.

Instead of taking a pause to indicate the tease, it is much more effective to rely on the other dynamics in the actor's kit, such as vocal color, movement, gesture, expression. This doesn't mean no hesitations; it means no unnecessary gaps. It means achieve your modest hesitations by flowing down and back up, not by chopping.

The frequency of Caesuras varies greatly. There are very few in the early scripts and they become more common as his writing matures. Here is an example from 1H6 1.4.39-56, a very early play. On the battlefield during the war, two warriors, Salisbury and Talbot meet unexpectedly after long separation. Salisbury prevails on Talbot to tell the story of his imprisonment.

He does and despite the intensity of the story, there is one Minor caesura in eighteen lines.

> With scoffs and scorns and contumelious taunts.
> In open market-place produc'd they me
> To be a public spectacle to all;
> Here, said they, is the terror of the French,
> The scarecrow that affrights our children so.
> Then broke I from the officers that led me,
> And with my nails digg'd stones out of the ground
> To hurl at the beholders of my shame.
> My grisly countenance made others fly,
> None durst come near for fear of sudden death.
> In iron walls they deem'd me not secure;
> So great fear of my name 'mongst them were spread
> That they suppos'd I could rend bars of steel,
> And spurn in pieces posts of adamant;
> Wherefore a guard of chosen shot I had
> That walk'd about me every minute while;
> And if I did but stir out of my bed,
> Ready they were to shoot me to the heart.

How simple can you get? One feminine ending, one inversion, and one inconsequential Caesura in 18 lines, conveying the raw vigor of this warrior brilliantly.

Now compare the 1H6 speech with this one from near the end of Shakespeare's career. No more simplicity. The Caesura has become a favorite variation. In this speech from *The Tempest*, 2.1.262—273 most of the 12 lines have Major Caesuras (10 in most modern editions, 9 in the *First Folio*, 11 by dramatic sense). Plus four Feminine Endings and two Inversions. Incredibly intricate.

> ... A space whose every cubit
> Seems to cry out, 'How shall that Claribel
> Measure us back to Naples? Keep in Tunis,
> And let Sebastian wake.' Say, this were death
> That now hath seized them; why, they were no worse
> Than now they are. There be that can rule Naples

> As well as he that sleeps; lords that can prate
> As amply and unnecessarily
> As this Gonzalo; I myself could make
> A chough of as deep chat. O, that you bore
> The mind that I do! What a sleep were this
> For your advancement! Do you understand me?

It takes a truly creative actor to fully exploit the opportunities offered by such rich verse since for every bit of advantage you gain, you are faced with an added challenge.

The biggest problem that comes along with the Caesura is the threat of losing the integrity of the line. Remember that everything depends on the audience or the reader being able to feel the beginning and end of every line. Lose that and you're doing prose. When you come face to face with speeches clocking 80% Major Caesuras, the task is formidable.

The job is toughest when lines are "run on"; that is, when there is no "stop" at the end of a line to help define it as the end. Consider this speech again. Where are the stops?

Unusual and extreme, isn't it? Every full stop except the last is in mid-line. Eleven of twelve lines are run on. And yet the through line is still basic Blank Verse and you want to keep a grip on it while exploiting the Variations.

Do not run-on the line just because there is an *enjambment* (the technical word for the continuation of the meaning of the sentence beyond the end of the verse line.)

Here's an example of a run-on line which would tempt you to not pause at the end of that verse line. Don't give into that temptation or you'll soon be acting prose.

> Being your slave, what should I do but tend
> Upon the hours and times of your desire?   SONN 57.1-2

When you run-on you erase the clear indications of the shape of the verse line. You do want a small pause at the end of the line and it is crucial that you justify the pause with subtext.

The shape of the line is the heart of the art.

Be rigorous in your application of this principle.

> **What can you do?**
> **As always, build a subtextual justification for everything.**
> **Take nothing for granted.**
> **Organic foundations hold. Mechanical foundations don't.**

> **Then be sure that this foundation generates the special energy and the pause required by a line ending and that the line attack has special vigor that defines the beginning of a line.**

THE SILENT BEAT IN MID-LINE

This variation is really a kind of Super Caesura but it is so special and so important that it deserves its own name and lots of attention.

A Silent Beat in Mid-Line is a short pause in mid-line generated technically by a missing syllable and dramatically by an abrupt event of importance. The pause and the event which cause it count, rhythmically, as a syllable. It exists to cover and to enhance a powerful moment of subtext or a major physical event.

To put it another way, THE SILENT BEAT is a slot provided by Shakespeare for you to insert the shortest of short lines, non-verbal but telling a big story nevertheless. Sometimes it is an entrance, sometimes a realization, often a surge of emotion, occasionally a moment when one topic ends and another begins. Always, it indicates a change, either of perception, intention, feeling, attitude, or a major decision.

You must justify your Silent Beat and both subtext and overt behavior must rationalize it for the audience. Play the change in approximately the time that would have been used by a spoken syllable; don't draw it out or you lose the beat. Everything that was said about fighting to maintain the integrity of the line in the section on Caesura applies here.

Silent Beats almost always substitute for relatively strong syllables. They most often serve as the second syllable of either the second or third foot. To indicate a Silent Beat in a text, put an **X** where the Silent Beat occurs.

These Silent Beats often occur in atypical lines **six feet** long but occasionally they are 5½ or 6½ foot lines.

Here is an example:

>   –   u / u   – / u   – /u   – / u – / u – / u
> Mur-der'd her kins- man. **X** O, tell me fri- ar, tell me   ROM 3.3.105

(6 ½ ft., fem., 1ˢᵗ inv., Silent Beat on heavy syllable of 3ʳᵈ ft.)

Shakespeare put this Silent Beat here to cover Romeo's sudden drawing of his dagger. There is always some such event at the Silent Beat. This is a six-foot line in *King Lear*:

>   u – / u   – / u – /u   – / u   – / u –
> Cor-de – lia leaves you. **X** I know you what you are.   KL 1.1.269

Cordelia begins to leave; then, at the Silent Beat, she stops abruptly, turns to her sisters, and speaks with complete candor.

Here, in *Timon of Athens* the Silent Beat enhances the moment of great tension when Timon dismisses Apemantus.

>   u   – / u   – / u – /u – / u   –
> Long live so, and so die. **X** I am quit.   TIM 4.3.398

In *Merchant of Venice*, the Silent Beat provides for the huge emotional impact when Bassanio opens the casket which reveals that he has won the hand of Portia and her fortune. They share the line; she speaks first.

>   u   – / u – /u – /
> For fear I surfeit. **X**
>
>   u   – / u –
>   What find I here?   MV 3.2.114

The Silent Beat is the primary device used to reveal Leontes' shattered mind in *A Winter's Tale*. He has three in five lines.

Here's one:

```
     u    – / u     – / u   – / u    – / u   –
    Hours minutes? Noon midnight? X And all eyes            WT 1.2.290
```

In *The Tempest*, the Silent Beat provides for a moment of physical action. "Father" is Prospero, the charmer. He speaks before the beat and Miranda speaks after.

```
       u    – / u  – / u      – / u
      Mine en'my has more pow'r. X      – / u    – / u
                                        O, dear father,         TEM 1.2.467
```

King Lear, in a brief moment of semi-lucidity near his end, sees through the fog of pain and madness and recognizes his faithful servant, Kent, whom he exiled but who followed him through all the terrors in disguise. The Silent Beat gives him a moment for the profound realization.

```
     u  – / u – / u     – / u    – / u    –
    This is a dull sight. X Are you not Kent?                KL 5.3.280
```

So simple, but, in the circumstances, so eloquent.

In *Coriolanus*, a messenger comes with bad news for Caius Martius. The Silent Beat defines the moment of impact, or realization of the importance of the news. I assume the beat is the moment when their gazes meet.

```
       u    – / u   – / u
      Where's Caius Martius?        – / u    – / u   – / u
                                    Here. X What's the matter?   COR 1.1.221
```

By the way, for Shakespeare, "What's the matter?" doesn't mean "What's wrong?" as it does for us. It means something like "What's the subject matter?"

THE SHARED LINE

This is one of Shakespeare's most effective devices. He splits one iambic pentameter line between two or more characters. This knits the lines together in a very effective way.

The desired effect only occurs when the actor speaking the second part of the line hears and builds upon the rhythm and tempo of the actor speaking the first part so that the integrity of the whole verse line structure is maintained. Do not take "meaningful pauses" at the break in the shared line. It undermines the rhythmic power completely. Take the tempo as it is handed to you. If you need to lead it elsewhere, gradually do that. But do not ignore the partial line which precedes yours and abruptly leap into another rhythmic world. It is shattering and distracting to the audience and disruptive to Shakespeare's strategy.

Many shared lines have 6 feet.

Here are examples of shared lines:

✓ ROMEO:	Farewell, my coz.		ROM 1.1.195
BENVOLIO:		Soft, I will go along.	ROM 1.1.195
✓ BENVOLIO:	For what, I pray thee?		ROM 1.2.52
ROMEO:		For your broken shin.	ROM 1.2.52
✓ ALBANY:	Well, you may fear too far.		KL 1.4.325
GONERIL:		Safer than trust too far. (6ft.)	KL 1.4.325

Note that Goneril's part of the line begins with an inversion, enhancing the feeling that she has interrupted him, snatching the conversation away from him.

✓ LEAR:	Out, varlet, from my sight!		KL 2.4.187
CORNWALL:		What means your grace?	KL 2.4.187

✓ ROMEO: That I might touch that cheek!		ROM 2.2.25
JULIET: Ay me!		ROM 2.2.25
ROMEO: She speaks!		ROM 2.2.25

```
✓ ROMEO:  That I might touch that cheek!                 ROM 2.2.25
   JULIET:                Ay me!                          ROM 2.2.25
   ROMEO:                         She speaks!             ROM 2.2.25

✓ JULIET:  Romeo!                                         ROM 2.2.167
   ROMEO:             My dove?                            ROM 2.2.167
   JULIET:                       At what o'clock tomorrow? ROM 2.2.167
```

Here is an example of a four-part shared line:

```
✓ HUBERT:  My lord.                                      KJ 3.3.66
   KING JOHN:      A grave.                              KJ 3.3.66
   HUBERT:                  He shall not live.           KJ 3.3.66
   KING JOHN:                            Enough.         KJ 3.3.66
```

What teamwork this takes!

Notice how the typography points out the Shared Lines. Any time your verse line doesn't begin at the left margin, your speech is part of a Shared Line.

This way of indicating Shared Lines, by the way, is the work of modern editors, not of Shakespeare and his typographers.

TESTIMONY OF THE SKILLED AND FAMOUS

"I can remember in performance the delight that Ben Kingsley and I enjoyed in forcing the pentameter through the shared lines. Picking up cues can become most magically truthful when lines are separated between characters."

Roger Rees, one of the best British actors

SHORT LINES: A SHAKESPEAREAN CODE FOR ACTORS

You will have noticed by now, clever reader, that not all of Shakespeare's lines are ten- or eleven-syllables long. As we have seen, a few are longer. Even more are shorter. He has given us lines from one to 8 (but never nine) syllables. Why?

You know that he wrote some of his wonderful stuff in other verse forms. Not much, but some. Many of these bits use shorter lines. Sometimes he did this to create special moods or to set different worlds apart or, as here, both.
This is Oberon in *A Midsummer Night's Dream*:

> What thou seest when thou dost wake,
> Do it for thy true love take,
> Love and languish for his sake.
> Be it ounce, or cat, or bear,
> Pard, or boar with bristled hair,
> In thy eye he shall appear
> When thou wak'st, it is thy dear.
> Wake when some vile thing is near.
>
> MND 2.2.33-40

This is a strong and rigidly regular verse form, almost the reverse of iambic pentameter. It is a basically trochaic beat with a consistent seven syllables to the line. No way could it sound as "natural" as iambic pentameter. Perfect to generate an aura of power and mystery for Oberon as he weaves his magical spell over Titania.

Amazingly, the same verse form can be flipped to a radically different mood, as it is in *A Midsummer Night's Dream*. The form that suited the sinister and mystical mood of Oberon's spell suits the bright and foolish capering of Puck. All you need to do is, as it were, take away the kettle drums, bass-baritone voice, and slower tempo of the Oberon moment and substitute a tambourine, a tenor, and a brisk tempo that tends toward accelerando, as here.

> Captain of our fairy band,
> Helena is here at hand;
> And the youth, mistook by me,
> Pleading for a lover's fee.
> Shall we their fond pageant see?
> Lord, what fools these mortals be!
>
> MND 3.2.110-115

But these delights are not what we're here to talk about. Sometimes the alternate verse forms are just experiments or playfulness. Sometimes they are much more.

We are here to consider the difficulties and the opportunities which appear when Shakespeare gets creative in new ways with iambic pentameter. I think of these as moments when Willie puts on his director's hat. Shakespeareans love to say that the Bard left us almost no stage directions, that most of those in our scripts were added by editors. Literally, that's true. The deeper truth, as J. L. Styan demonstrated so well in his *Shakespeare's Stagecraft*, is that the text itself is loaded with instructions for actors and directors; strong implications which can be overlooked or ignored only at great cost. Short lines are among the most valuable of these.

Shakespeare uses the Short Line to tell the actor to pause. The number of syllables omitted from the line suggests the approximate length of the pause.

When you see what we call a "Short Line" of blank verse, you're not really seeing a short line; more meaningfully, you're seeing a full line, only part of which is audible. It is important not to throw away the unspoken part. Don't intrude the next line into that precious space.

Here are some of the common situations in which Short Lines appear, set in a brief context. I've given my own labels to these.

THE CALL: a character, usually relatively important, calls for the attention of a group. The Short Line is The Call. The pause which follows intensifies the reaction and movement of the disputants whose hash King Richard II is about to settle. It also allows for the trumpet flourish which has been misplaced by modern editors. The flourish has been called for, but not placed, in the dialogue. King Richard speaks:

Let them lay by their helmets and their spears,
And both return back to their chairs again.
Withdraw with us, and let the trumpets sound
While we return the dukes what we decree.
Draw near,
And list what with our council we have done.   R2 1.2.119-124

You might be tempted by the comma ending the Short Line plus the "and" beginning the next line to knit the two lines together tightly. Don't do it. You'll lose a great moment of tension.

WOW!: when a sudden, startling piece of news emerges, the silent moment covers the impact. Here is a good example from *Measure for Measure*. Claudio is imprisoned, condemned to death for fornication. He has sent his sister, Isabella, a novice nun, to the head man, Angelo, to beg for mercy. Angelo, the supposed righteous man, says "yes," if Isabella will sleep with him. She assumes that Claudio values her virtue more than his life. She comes to his cell to tell him he will die tomorrow.

ISABELLA
Lord Angelo, having affairs to heaven,   (fem. End, 3rd inv.)
Intends you for his sweet ambassador,
Where you shall be an everlasting leiger;   (fem. End)
Therefore your best appointment make with speed,
Tomorrow you set on.

CLAUDIO
Is there no remedy?   (fem. End, mid-v)

ISABELLA
None, but such remedy as, to save a head,   (mid-v)
To cleave a heart in twain.

CLAUDIO
But is there any?   (fem. End)

ISABELLA

Yes, brother, you may live;   (3 ft.)
There is a devilish mercy in the judge,   MM 3.1.56-64

Think of the moment: Isabella comes to Claudio who is wracked with fear. She tells him he will die tomorrow, throwing him deeper into the pit, then, unexpectedly she throws him a rope of hope. The impact must be terrible. Shakespeare has indicated it and provided for it by shortening the key line. Go with him. Take the intense pause he's given you.

HANGING ON: Look at this second bit from *Measure for Measure*. Claudio speaks with the Duke, the true ruler, who is disguised as a friar to observe the character of his dukedom.

DUKE

So then you hope of pardon from Lord Angelo?

CLAUDIO

The miserable have no other medicine
But only hope: (2 ft.)
I've hope to live, and am prepar'd to die: MM 3.1.1-4

How would you interpret this? Claudio is under terrific pressure and he's not a strong man. The friar's message is "prefer death; life has nothing to offer." Why do you think he needs that hesitation? I would say that this is an example of HANGING ON, trying to keep a grip on yourself, which requires a pause now and then.

THE CHALLENGE: the first of two Short Lines for the Dauphin (heir to the French throne) in *Henry V*, 3.5.9, seems to be an example of THE CHALLENGE, after which one waits for a response. In this case, the Dauphin (or, as Shakespeare called him, the Dolphin) and a gang of major nobles storm onstage, ranting about the lack of French military response to the English army rampaging across France under the leadership of Henry V.

DAUPHIN

> O Dieu vivant! Shall a few sprays of us,
> The emptying of our fathers' luxury,
> Our scions, put in wild and savage stock,
> Spirit up so suddenly into the clouds,
> And overlook their grafters?   (3.5 ft.)

This Short Line is the last line of his speech. Played right, the unspoken part of the line can be the most powerful part.

A few lines later, the Dolphin's rant is in a still higher gear, he tries to take it to the limit. Lord after Lord has spoken of the disgrace of inaction. The Dolphin leaps into the high-decibel melee with yet uglier predictions, starting with a Short Line.

> By faith and honor,   (2.5 ft.)
> Our madams mock at us and plainly say
> Our mettle is bred out, and they will give
> Their bodies to the lust of English youth
> To new-store France with bastard warriors.   H5 3.5.27-31

What would you call this kind of short line? What work does it do to justify the shortness and pause? What does the shortness of the line tell you about how it should be spoken?

Here is another from *Henry V* which can be taken two ways, one routine, one definitely not. On the field at the famed battle of Agincourt, where a small, rag-tag English army has defeated a much larger, richer French force, Henry gets some battlefield intel:

> But hark! What new alarum is this same?
> The French have reinforced their scattered men:
> Then every soldier kill his prisoners,
> Give the word through.
> *They go*   H5 4.6.36-39

This could be a simple example of THE EXIT Short Line. Or it could be a very strong version of WOW! As the soldiers react with shock to the order to kill their prisoners. Your take on this whole ambiguous show will determine which you choose.

> **There are many reasons for Short Lines.**
>
> **Each one needs to be justified individually
> with full consideration of the whole role and the whole play.**

One last set of examples from a scene that is pretty tough to scan. It includes verse, prose, short lines, and shared lines. It's from *Hamlet*'s first moments.

Here is the way it was laid out in the First Folio of Shakespeare's works with spelling modernized. Francisco and Barnardo, two sentinels, enter from separate spaces. They are spooked because of recent experiences on this platform and the general tone of activity in Denmark.

BAR.	Who's there?
FRAN.	Nay answer me. Stand and unfold yourself.
BAR.	Long live the King.
FRAN.	Barnardo?
BAR.	He.
FRAN.	You come most carefully upon your hour.
BAR.	'Tis now struck twelve, get thee to bed Francisco.
FRAN.	For this relief much thanks. 'Tis bitter cold, And I am sick at heart.
BAR.	Have you had quiet guard?
FRAN.	Not a mouse stirring.

BAR.	Well, goodnight. If you do meet Horatio and Marcellus, the Rivals of
	     my watch, bid them make haste.
	     Enter Horatio and Marcellus

Short Lines: A Shakespearean Code for Actors

FRAN.	I think I hear them. Stand; who's there?	
HOR.	Friends to this ground.	
MAR.	And liege-men to the Dane.	
FRAN.	Give you good night.	
MAR.	O farewell honest Soldier, who hath reliev'd you?	
FRAN.	Barnardo hath my place. Give you goodnight.	
	Exit Francisco	
MAR.	Hola Barnardo.	
BAR.	Say, what is Horatio there?	
HOR.	A piece of him.	
BAR.	Welcome *Horatio*, welcome good Marcellus.	
MAR.	What, has this thing appeared again tonight?	
BAR.	I have seen nothing.	HAM 1.1.2-22

As you see, the typesetters of Shakespeare's time (and perhaps William himself) didn't do us the favor of lining things up to reveal the shape of the verse.

PAUSE HERE AND TEST YOURSELF

Before you go on to see how I would reorganize the text to reveal the verse intent more clearly, try to do it yourself. Move the text around as appropriate and describe the character experiences which justify your changes. Then compare your version with mine and see if we're on the same track, particularly in the case of Short Lines.

OK, did you get through that alright? It's true; there are a few oddities in it. Does yours look anything like this? (For simplicity and conservation of effort, I'm leaving speech headings out.)

Who's there?   (*Short Line; fear and caution in the darkness; the wrong person made the call.*)

Nay, Answer me. Stand and unfold yourself.   (*3rd ft. inv.*)

Long live the King!
Barnardo?
He.   *(It is very tempting to make the first of this three-line group ["Long live ..."] a ShortLine justified by Francisco's need for a suspicious moment when he hears the password. The next two lines, however, kill that notion. There's no justification for slowing down the movement from "Barnardo" to "He." I feel it's either all three Short or none so I declare these three lines to be prose and I ask the actors playing these two to spill the lines out quickly, in relief, once the password indicates relative safety.)*

You come most carefully upon your hour.   *(stock line)*
'Tis now struck twelve. Get thee to bed Francisco.   *(stock fem.)*
For this relief much thanks. 'Tis bitter cold,   *(stock line)*
And I am sick at heart.   *(Short Line – Shall they bring up the fearful topic of the ghost visitations? They feel each other out. Start indirectly.)*

Have you had quiet guard?
        Not a mouse stirring.   *(shared line –fem. End – 4th inv.)*

Well, good night.   *(You might be tempted to call this a Short Line but it won't scan. It's prose.)*

(You can do the same thing you would want to with a Short Line: Barnabus speaks the words, Francisco starts to leave. Barnabus feels the rush of fearful solitude and jumps in with the two full lines which follow, a call for help.)

If you do meet Horatio and Marcellus,   *(stock fem.)*
The rivals of my watch, bid them make haste.   *(stock line)*
I think I hear them. Stand ho! Who is there?   *(stock line)*
Friends to this ground.
        And liegemen to the Dane.   *(1st inv. – shared line)*
Give you good night.

Short Lines: A Shakespearean Code for Actors

    O farewell honest soldier. (*shared line – fem. End –
              Don't take this "farewell" as routine.
              Take the "O" which precedes it as an
              indicator of strong feeling. Marcellus
              knows about the ghost.*)
Who hath relieved you?
    Barnardo hath my place. (*6 ft. line*)
Give you good night.   *Exit Francisco*
    Holla Barnardo!
        Say – (*3-way shared line*)
What, is Horatio here?
    A piece of him. (*stock shared line*)
Welcome, Horatio, welcome, good Marcellus. (*fem. End. – 1ˢᵗ inv.*)
What, has this thing appear'd again tonight? (*stock line*)
I have seen nothing. (*Short Line – Finally the big topic is
             on the table. Horatio, the "expert" of
             the group is here for business, and being
             an intellectual is skeptical. He deflates
             their fear with his mockery. This short
             line gives Horatio time for his "I told
             you so" laugh.*)

This is one man's interpretation at one point in time, not fact, particularly my justifications of the short lines. The important thing is to *have* a justification for every choice that fits with every other justification of your role, your scene, and the whole script.

Don't miss the powerful implication of the Short Line. If Shakespeare's Short-Line code tells you where to pause, he clearly doesn't want you to do a lot of pausing elsewhere.

The Short Line is one of Shakespeare's most effective special techniques. All you have to do to cooperate is take the pause and fully justify it. If you run on to the next line, his special effect is lost.

THE LILT

The Lilt will help maintain the integrity and clarify the structure of the line.

The Lilt is my name for an inflection we all use when we want to hesitate before our thought is finished, to tantalize our listeners by cuing them that what we're about to say is very interesting, or when we are uncertain, when we'd rather not say what we're about to say, etc. (For actors, the listeners are other characters, except when we play soliloquies, in which case the audience is the listener.)

> **We use the Lilt at the end of each verse line except where the end of the thought falls at the end of the line.**

> **When we Lilt, we "suspend" our sentence, we swing our pitch up slightly; that is, we do just the opposite of what we do when we want our listener to know that we are at the end of an idea. And we hesitate, however briefly, because we know that this suspenseful withholding of our thoughts makes people listen more eagerly.**

The actual length and shape of the hesitation depends, as does everything, on meanings, purposes, attitudes, emotions, *et cetera*.

Without some form of the Lilt, the **necessary brief pauses at the end of each line** have the opposite effect. They lessen interest by confusing the listener about the shape of your thought. Pauses are too mechanical without the Lilt. The Lilt is too mechanical without appropriate **subtext** to require it. This means that we are obliged to find a **subtextual need** to hesitate and to suspend. We begin working on the Lilt because we know it is a technical necessity; we end by using the Lilt because only it will clarify our meanings and spellbind our listeners.

> **There are hundreds of different nuances of thought and feeling that may justify the Lilt, so there are hundreds of different shapes the Lilt may take. Before lilting, find the nuance of thought which requires it.**

Danger Points

Danger Point 1: In real life, we all know intuitively when and how to Lilt. We do it all the time. But when we start working with Shakespeare, most of us lose that understanding.

Perhaps it's because too often we act Shakespeare with incomplete subtext. He requires as profound and rich an inner life as any writer. He requires honesty.

Danger Point 2: Something about the visual shape of a verse line encourages new performers of Shakespeare to do just the opposite of the Lilt: their music is constantly inflecting downward, pulled by the line end, it says "finished" in the middle of the character's thought. This produces leaden and confusing speech and, before long, boredom.

The solution is to know exactly what you mean,

truly mean what you say,

and integrate that with the commands of the verse form.

Make a special effort to master the Lilt.

The Lilt lifts, vitalizes, clarifies, and impels.

LILT EXERCISES

Here is a 10½-line speech by Hamlet. Only one of the verse lines is end-stopped. He is so unsettled, he can't touch down to the ground in any normal way. The playwright has given him verse shaped brilliantly to keep him aloft, tossed by wild winds. When he does come down, he crashes in mid-line. Twice he lands so violently that it causes **Silent Beats**. Use this exercise to refine your ability to meaningfully sustain a speech at length without inserting unwanted and damaging stops. Find the meaning of each lilt. Keep the mid-line stops and Silent Beats from obscuring the true starts and ends of the verse lines. If you can do this, the listener should become almost as unsettled as Hamlet. (HAM 1.2.135)

> Fie on't, ah fie, 'tis an unweeded garden ⌒
> That grows to seed; things rank and gross in nature ⌒
> Possess it merely. **X** That it should come to this!   (6 ft.)
> But two months dead—nay, not so much, not two—
> So excellent a King, that was to this ⌒
> Hyperion to a satyr, **X** so loving to my mother ⌒   (7½ ft.)
> That he might not beteem the winds of heaven ⌒
> Visit her face too roughly. Heav'n and earth, ⌒
> Must I remember? Why she would hang on him ⌒
> As if increase of appetite had grown ⌒
> By what it fed on;

In this scene, Ophelia describes Hamlet's distracted state. (HAM 2.1.87-96)

> He took me by the wrist and held me hard.
> Then goes he to the length of all his arm, ⌒
> And with his other hand thus o'er his brow ⌒
> He falls to such perusal of my face ⌒
> As 'a would draw it. **X** Long stayed he so.
> At last, a little shaking of mine arm ⌒
> And thrice his head thus waving up and down, ⌒
> He raised a sigh so piteous and profound ⌒
> As it did seem to shatter all his bulk ⌒
> And end his being.

The Lilt

TESTIMONY OF THE WISE AND FAMOUS

"As he was a happy imitator of nature, was a most gentle expresser of it. His mind and hand went together: And what he thought, he uttered with that easinesse, that wee have scarse received from him a blot in his papers .... his wit can no more lie hid, then it could be lost. Reade him, therefore; and againe, and againe: And if then you doe not like him, surely you are in some manifest danger not to understand him."

1623, by John Heminge and Henrie Condell, fellow actors, friends, and editors of the First Folio of Shakespeare's plays

THERE ARE EXCEPTIONS: E.G. ACCENTUAL VERSE

Not all of Shakespeare's verse was iambic pentameter. Blank verse is one kind of **SYLLABIC/ACCENTUAL VERSE.** (Which means we count the number of syllables and say where the accents go within the feet.) **Shakespeare also tried his hand a few times at an ACCENTUAL VERSE that was not Syllabic. He wrote lines with four relatively strong beats and no rule about the numbter of syllables in the line.**

This form is more like music: imagine that each strong beat is the one-beat of a bar of music. Any syllables that come before the first strong emphasis are like "pickup notes" in music. The "no-short-syllables rule" doesn't apply so rigidly in this purely Accentual form. It is a light, bright, and always comic style. Here is an example from *Comedy of Errors,* 3.1.12. I have underlined and bolded the four major accents in each line. Try to keep the rhythms of the four more emphatic syllables steady, as in music.

E. Dromio	That you <u>beat</u> me at the <u>mart</u>, I <u>have</u> your hand to <u>show</u>; If the <u>skin</u> were <u>parch</u>ment and the <u>blows</u> you gave were <u>ink</u>, Your <u>own</u> hand<u>writ</u>ing would <u>tell</u> you what I <u>think</u>.
E. Antipholus	I <u>think</u> thou art an <u>ass</u>.
E. Dromio	Marry, <u>so</u> it doth ap<u>pear</u> By the <u>wrongs</u> I <u>suf</u>fer, and the <u>blows</u> I <u>bear</u>. I should <u>kick</u>, being <u>kick'd</u>. and <u>be</u>ing at that <u>pass</u>, You would <u>keep</u> from my <u>heels</u>, and be<u>ware</u> of an <u>ass</u>.
E. Antipholus	Y'are <u>sad</u>, Signior <u>Bal</u>thazar, pray <u>God</u> our <u>cheer</u> May <u>an</u>swer my good <u>will</u> and <u>your</u> good welcome <u>here</u>.

There Are Exceptions: E.g. Accentual Verse

Balthazar   I <u>hold</u> your dainties <u>cheap</u>, sir, and <u>your</u> good welcome <u>dear</u>.

E. Antipholus   <u>O</u> Signior <u>Bal</u>thazar, <u>either</u> at flesh or <u>fish</u>,
         A <u>ta</u>ble full of <u>wel</u>come makes <u>scarce</u> one dainty <u>dish</u>.

Balthazar   Good <u>meat</u>, sir, is <u>com</u>mon; that <u>every</u> churl a<u>ffords</u>.

E. Antipholus   And <u>wel</u>come more <u>com</u>mon, for that's <u>no</u>thing but <u>words</u>.

It may help to see a few of these lined up somewhat like music:

I /**hold** your dainties	/**cheap** sir and	/**your** good welcome	/**dear**
/**O** Signior	/**Bal**-thasar	/**ei**ther at flesh or	/**fish**
a /**ta**-ble full of	/**wel**-come makes	/**scarce** one dainty	/**dish**

Notice that the units here, the equivalent of a **Foot** in syllabic verse or a **Measure** in music, may have any number of syllables but, as in music, the **Length** of each unit is the same. The tempo may increase or decrease but time flows, as in all kinds of verse. There are no abrupt shifts or chops.

This kind of **Accentual Verse** could very easily be done to a drum beat or to music. It could even be done as a soft-shoe dance.

AND WHILE WE'RE AT IT, ANOTHER SYLLABIC FORM

Shakespeare was an experimenter. In his earliest plays, he tried many other forms. When he uses alternate forms in his mature plays, it is for very special situations. One of his favorites is the seven-syllable line, often used for songs:

    Who is Silvia? What is she,/That all our swains commend her?   TGV 4.2.38

Note that this alternates Trochaic and Iambic groups:

– u – u – u – / u – u – u – u

Or, in another song, the same pattern with an added masculine ending:

    Tell me where is fancy bred,/Or in the heart, or in the head?   MV 3.2.63

Sometimes his seven-syllable lines are ritualistic chants. Seven-syllable Trochaic lines are favored by the Witches in *Macbeth* 1.3.19:

    – u / – u / –   u / –
    Sleep shall neither night nor day
    Hang upon his penthouse lid;
    He shall live a man forbid;
    Weary sev'nights, nine times nine,
    Shall he dwindle, peak, and pine;
    Though his bark cannot be lost,
    Yet it shall be tempest-toss'd.

And While We're At It, Another Syllabic Form

Such forms are much less subtle than **Blank Verse** and should be played broadly. The ritualistic or theatrical or comical qualities should not be subverted by an effort to make them sound as natural as Blank Verse.

Almost always these seven-syllable lines will be intermixed with lines of other lengths. Macbeth's Witches have several six-syllable and several eight-syllable lines. Take nothing for granted. Scan carefully and **always look for the dramatic reason underlying the shifts in verse form.**

Occasionally Will wrote **iambic tetrameter**, a verse line of **four iambic feet.** Here is a sample from *Pericles,* Chorus.4.5, spoken by Gower, the narrator/chorus figure:

> Now <u>to</u> Ma<u>ri</u>na <u>bend</u> your <u>mind</u>
> Whom <u>our</u> fast-<u>grow</u>ing <u>scene</u> must <u>find</u>
> At <u>Thar</u>sis. <u>And</u> by <u>Cle</u>on <u>trained</u>
> In <u>mu</u>sic's <u>let</u>ters, <u>who</u> hath <u>gain</u>'d
> Of <u>e</u>du<u>ca</u>tion <u>all</u> the <u>grace</u>,
> Which <u>makes</u> her <u>both</u> the <u>heart</u> and <u>place</u>
> Of <u>gen</u>eral <u>won</u>der. <u>But</u> a<u>lack</u>,
> That <u>mon</u>ster <u>Env</u>y, <u>oft</u> the <u>wrack</u>
> Of <u>earned</u> <u>praise</u>, Ma<u>ri</u>na's <u>life</u>
> <u>Seeks</u> to take <u>off</u> by <u>trea</u>son's <u>knife</u>.

See how much more artificial this feels. The combination of the four-foot line with the rhyming couplets has that effect and it is a very useful device in the right place. The four-foot line is inherently less "natural" sounding to us than the five and that's why iambic pentameter became the basic form of verse drama. There are many other alternate forms. When you find them, think of them as special spices for special dishes and make the most of them.

Shakespeare's Verse: A User's Manual

> **TESTIMONY OF THE INCREDIBLY TALENTED AND INFLUENTIAL**
>
> Truth . . . speak the truth, though the verse will not entirely take care of itself. Shakespeare knew what he was doing; he put the rhythms there and he didn't wish them to be ignored.
>
> Laurence Olivier, the great Shakespearean actor of the 20th century

Here is a very odd, regular form for a Puck spell:

On the ground	– u –
Sleep sound	– –
I'll apply,	– u –
[To] your eye,	– u –
Gentle lover, remedy	– u – u – u –
When thou wak'st,	– u –
Thou tak'st	– –
True delight	– u –
In the sight	– u –
Of thy former lady's eye;	– u – u – u –
And the country proverb known,	– u – u – u –
That every man should take his own,	u – u – u – u –
In your waking shall be shown	– u – u – u –
Jack shall have Jill;	– u u –
Nought shall be ill;	– u u –

The man shall have his mare again, and all shall be well.   (prose)

MND 3.2.448

And While We're At It, Another Syllabic Form

TESTIMONY OF THE INCREDIBLY TALENTED AND INFLUENTIAL

Lord Lawrence said that Orson Welles "had everything for Othello, everything except the breath. He didn't go into training, and after 'Like the Pontic sea' he had to pause . . . When all is said and done, for Othello you need the breath, the lungs . . . You need the self-discipline and the rhythm. At the basis of everything is rhythm."

Lawrence Olivier, the great Othello.

WHAT SHAPES THE WAY WE SPEAK A LINE?

The "music" of our speech communicates much more than the words themselves. These are the things which shape our music:

THE MEANINGS: This is the most important factor. "**Meaning**" includes **what the words say** and **why we say them** and **our attitude** toward our listeners and toward what we are saying.

Meaning shapes our speech according to **rules of the language** and **stylistic habits of our culture**. Meaning shapes speech in Shakespeare in exactly the same way it shapes speech in any play. But the actor in a period play must face the challenge of discovering the attitudes of a different time, place, and, often, class.

Our most abundant and difficult meanings are in our **SUBTEXT**. Subtext has tremendous influence on the **nuances** of our speech. The words tell what we're saying; the Subtext, as revealed by the music of our speech and the dance of our body, tells what we are experiencing and generates what we say and do.

> SUBTEXT: everything that happens in the character's mind which is not directly expressed in the text. Not just words; images, muscular flow, all that registers, ever so lightly, in consciousness.

In Shakespeare, the music of the verse is never in conflict with the text or Subtext.

They support each other fully.

The verse rhythm provides our best clues to the meanings.

The verse rhythms lay a foundation on which the expression of meanings is built. The verse says "this must be done and that must not" but it does not tell us how to say the line.

Rhythm provides a framework which our meanings bring to life.

SCANSION ONE

**The artist begins work on the verse
by scanning each line.**

That is, by finding the pattern of greater and lesser emphasis in the lines. By seeing how a line conforms to and diverges from the standard line.

> **To *Scan* a line is to recognize its rhythmic shape.**
>
> **The process of scanning is called *Scansion* or *Metrical Analysis*.**
>
> **Scanning a line is like learning the melody and rhythm of a song.**

Let's try scanning a few lines, starting with this famous speech of Mercutio's from *Romeo and Juliet* (ROM 1.4.53-93):

O then I see Queen Mab hath been with you.

When you're new to the scansion game, it's difficult to keep track of your syllable and emphasis count. I have convinced myself that one of the main reasons God gave us five fingers was to simplify our scanning of pentameter. I recommend, at the start of this work, that you very carefully monitor your scans by tapping one finger at a time, on even beats only (that is, on relatively heavier syllables), until you run out of fingers on one hand.

At first, you will find this much more difficult than it sounds. You may find yourself tapping the same finger again and again and therefore getting no foot count. You may tap randomly and lose track of emphases or miss the variations. Keep at it; be strict with yourself. Don't give in to the frustration that almost everyone feels.

It is worth getting good control of the tap at the beginning so that you have a scan you can count on. The tapping system is like training wheels on your bicycle: awkward but necessary for most of us at the start. Our goal, of course, is to absorb the blank verse rhythm so profoundly that counting becomes superfluous; we simply feel the rightness or wrongness of a line as we hear a right or wrong note in music. We're not ready to perform verse until speaking a line with a wrong emphasis, or with a syllable too many or too few, jerks us up like hitting a pothole in the road.

As you tap the line out, speak it exaggeratedly, mechanically. Don't try to make it sound good. You're looking for the things that *don't* fit the stock pattern, not the things that *do*. If there are variations or unexpected pronunciation shifts, you want them to jump out at you as problems to be solved.

Now, tap out Mercutio's line. Did you come out even? What kind of line did you think it is? I hope you said "stock" because that's the way it looks to me: ten syllables; five iambic feet. I see no reason to declare any variations. Occasionally, someone suggests to me that we might invert the first foot. I'm convinced that those "O"s which begin lines, though they are big, are never bigger than the following syllable but rather serve as wonderful warm-ups which sweep into the driving phrases which follow.

Here is the next line. Tap away.

> She is the fairies midwife, and she comes

Did you find another stock line? Or did you have an urge to invert the first foot? Many do. I don't. See the section called "The Personal Pronoun Trap" for a sample. There is no convincing reason to invert. In this case, "she" needs no special attention. Inverting the foot would draw undue attention to "she" and away from "fairies midwife." But this is a subtle matter. My "is" will be *slightly* more emphatic than my "she." So, I say this is another stock line. Yet, I admit, it is a judgment call.

> **I urge you to adopt this conservative principle: invert only when you have a compelling reason. When you do, make the most of it.**

Four lines later, Mercutio says,

> Over men's noses as they lie asleep

No doubt you found something wrong here. You started tapping and you heard yourself say "o-VER." You tried to make that work. You couldn't. You told yourself there were two possible explanations: either Shakespeare pronounced "over" differently than we do or the first foot of this line is inverted. We'll deal with the issue of pronunciation in detail later. For now, I'll tell you that he didn't say "o-VER." What we have here is a first foot inversion. If you wanted to mark your script according to my system, you would do this:

– u /
O-ver men's noses as they lie asleep.

Mark only the variations or your page will be too cluttered to read.

Just to give you a taste of complexities to come, here, two lines earlier, is a tougher puzzle, particularly for Americans:

> On the forefinger of an alderman,

You probably felt two bumps in your road: one on the first foot and one on the second. Do you think the simple solution is to invert the first two feet?
I can't go with you on that. The first foot, yes; second foot, no. If, as a diligent Shakespearean, you sensed the awkwardness of the line with first and second foot inversions and jumped online to check the concordance at www.Shakespeareswords.com on the off chance that

Shakespeare's habit was to say "fore-FIN-ger," you were disappointed to find that Will only used the word once in a verse line so there's no evidence at that site.

How did I decide against the second foot inversion? I did that concordance chase and scanned all of the hundreds of compound words like "forefinger." What I found was that, though the American habit is to emphasize the syllable *before* the word joint, Shakespeare much more frequently emphasized the syllable after the joint.

The other reason to reject the second foot inversion is the fact that **there are no instances of two inverted feet in a row in all of Shakespeare.** Why?

It would crush the Swoop, turning one of the most beautiful, powerful moments into a clunker. That's why, in context, the line sounds so awkward when read with the first two feet inverted. So we call this line "first inversion, masculine ending."

    –   u   /
On the fore**fin**ger of an alderman,

Skip down to line 62 in Mercutio's speech.

    Her wagon-spokes made of long spinners' legs,

What do you want to do with this? Where do you feel the bump in the road? Probably at the relatively emphatic "of." Sometimes it might be appropriate to let this be the more emphatic syllable but here it feels a bit odd. What excuse do we have to invert the foot? Does the line mean more if we do? Is the idea more fully energized if we invert? Yes and yes. Mercutio is trying to dazzle his friends; this rhythm seems to lend itself better to that purpose. An inversion seems legit. This is one of those judgment calls. Not necessary but OK. Label it "3rd foot inversion, masculine ending" if you prefer.

              /   –   u   /
Her wagon-spokes **made** of long spinners' legs,

Try this Theseus line from *Midsummer Night's Dream*

    Merry and tragical? Tedious and brief?

You hit your first bump at "Merry," right? You probably wasted little time there, deciding quickly that the pronunciation of "Merry" required a 1st foot inversion, rejecting the possibility that Shakespeare might say "mare-EE" as unlikely. Your next problem came with the 4th foot where you found an extra syllable and some awkward emphases. What did you do about that? Were you inspired to try compressing "tedious" into two syllables – TEE-djuss? If so, everything fell into place for you. You found that you had an exciting line with 1st and 4th foot inversions and a compression. (For an explanation of Compression, see page 88.)

       – u /   / – u /
    Merry and tragical? **Te**dious and brief?

And there you have a simple intro to Scansion. We'll deal with more complicated Scansion problems later.

This wasn't so hard. Except for, maybe, those little difficulties with "forefinger" and "tedious." If that's all there is to Scansion, no problem.

BUT THERE'S A CATCH

A big one. I stacked the deck with easy lines, lines with language that hasn't changed significantly since Shakespeare's time. The harsh truth is that if you master Shakespeare's basic system and his variations, then pick up a published Shakespeare script and read it as it is printed, you will massacre the verse. Pick a favorite role and try to scan it; you will find that many of your lines don't fit the system as I described it.

Now, before you decide that either Shakespeare didn't obey his own rules or that I got it all wrong, stop for a moment and consider that 400-plus years have passed and the language has changed. Evolution of the language has shortened many words, lengthened others, changed the emphasis pattern of others. Also, modern editors have "corrected" Shakespeare's spelling and punctuation in ways that have lost many of his indications of pronunciation. If you read these texts normally, you will speak the wrong number of syllables and you will put many emphases in the wrong places. Such changes destroy the verse rhythm. You'll be speaking prose.

If we're to speak verse, we have to accommodate those changes. Fortunately, we can do that in almost every case without confusing or distracting the audience. In almost every case, we can get the many aesthetic values out of using the rhythmic features of Shakespeare's pronunciation without the audience consciously noticing that we're doing it.

Another reason we often scan incorrectly is that the "awe factor" many of us experience when we work with Shakespeare causes us to adopt a formality which leads us to use longer forms of many words which we would normally elide. We say "GEN-er-AL" instead of our normal "GEN'-ral," resulting in bad rhythm and stiff feeling. Shakespeare typically used the shorter forms, unless he needed an extra syllable.

Shakespeare wrote his scripts for actors he knew. They spoke as he did and he was present in the theatre to correct their rhythm if they slipped. One of the things he counted on was the actors' understanding of **Elision** (rhymes with *decision*). Elision is the omission of an unemphatic vowel or syllable.

Example: when Shakespeare used "Many a" as the first words in a verse line, he wanted it pronounced as we ordinarily do, MEN-ee-UH; but when "many a" is used in any other position in a line, it is **elided** (that is, made an **elision**) and pronounced MEN-yuh.

There are thousands of elisions in Shakespeare and very few of them are typographically indicated. The same is true of contractions. It's up to you to find them.

Many of Shakespeare's words are pronounced more briefly than modern editors have spelled them in the texts. For example, "even" is almost always spoken as one syllable, "een"; "spirit" is most often spoken "speert." Two of the hardest ones, "heaven" and "seven" are almost always one-syllable words.

So, there is much to learn about Shakespeare's language. Fortunately, it is not necessary to master the whole vocabulary, though that would be ideal. If you dig deeply enough, you will begin to see patterns which will improve your skills as a scansion problem solver. As you work to develop your personal mastery of the language, there is a rapidly growing archive of resources to help you along the way.

- For actors, best of all is a truly knowledgeable director or speech coach. There are precious few of these but more every year.

- A good concordance (listing of every use of every word, in context). To find the shape of a word, scan it in all of its verse appearances. My favorite hard copy concordance is the one-volume version of Marvin Spevack's *Harvard Concordance to Shakespeare*. The most convenient is David and Ben Crystal's online version, Shakespeareswords.com.

- Two older books are useful and can still be found: check out Helge Kokeritz's *Shakespeare's Pronunciation* which is mostly accurate on words that are longer and shorter than we're used to and E.A. Abbott's *A Shakespearian Grammar*.

- A script properly prepared for production, edited for the actor, which reveals the crucial verse information typographically. Of these, I know of none except the nine I have prepared for my own productions. Learn more at: www.ShakespearesVerse-UsersManual.com

Until you acquire these resources, your best friends are your rigor and ingenuity as a scanner.

Some actors, when they hear of "een" and "speert" and one-syllable "heaven" begin to worry about alienating the audience by sounding "antique." Do not fear. If you speak them easily and if you mean what you say, most of these changes are not noticed by the audiences. If you are honest, the audience is following the story and is hooked on it. If you are working the rhythm, then the rhythm is doing its subliminal magic and the proper union of the music and the meaning is making everything clear; not just your words but the workings of your soul.

> **In the sections that follow, I have given you an introduction to the most common language patterns that might trip you up as you begin scanning. I have provided substantial samples of each type of word that might give you trouble. I have chosen not to use the formal, more precise International Phonetic Alphabet because I want to reach many people who aren't trained in the IPA. Instead, I have used the "common man's" pronunciation guide, which, I hope, is clear to all.**
>
> **The pronunciations I give are, I believe, authoritative in the matter of number of syllables and placement of emphases. I can't claim as much for the vowel sounds. We have much less evidence for vowels and, at any rate, my goal was to give the most recognizable, non-regional, contemporary American-English sounds. My apologies to the speakers of British-English. They will, by the way, find that several of the words I call "odd-emphasis words" don't sound odd to them at all.**

I want to make very clear that I am not advocating or teaching a full recreation of Shakespeare's speech. That noble project is now in the hands of David Crystal, the same man who created ShakespearesWords.com and has actually guided "original pronunciation" productions at the Globe Theatre in London. David's son Ben has guided a project to record large chunks of Shakespeare's work in what they take to be the Original Pronunciation. I am somewhat persuaded of the accuracy of their vowel findings. Unfortunately, the recent recordings based on the Crystal work reveal that their extensive research did not include study of the verse-rhythm demands and most of the old errors persist there. We're still stuck with RO-mee OH and JOO-lee-EHT.

Useful work on Original Pronunciation has been done by Paul Meier and he has written about it in his good book, *Voicing Shakespeare*.

At any rate, I have no aim and make no claim to deal with the full scope of Shakespeare's poetic achievement. I'm here to lay the foundation stone.

> **My goal is to get these plays back into verse and the heart of that project is to get people speaking the right number of syllables with the emphases in the right places. The two keys to that work are to understand the basic system and to know enough about the pronunciation to facilitate your problem-solving as a scanner.**

This is not the whole story of Shakespeare's poetry but it is the essential foundation. Brilliant men like John Barton, Peter Hall, Peter Groves and Adrian Noble have written insightfully about other aspects of Shakespeare's genius. None has written sufficiently and accessibly about these two keys.

First, let's take a look at a few lines which illustrate a moderate degree of the kind of difficulty I'm talking about.

Back to the same speech of Mercutio's, lines 61 and 63.

Time out a' mind the fairies coachmakers.

The cover of the wings of grasshoppers,

Do you find these troublesome? Maybe you are tempted to invert "Time out" but you remember that I urged you not to invert unless you have a compelling reason and you can't really see one here other than that "time" is a noun at the start of the line. Don't do it. If anything, "out a' mind" is slightly more needful of emphasis. But, anyway, what bothered you most about these lines were the endings: "coachmakers" and "grasshoppers" just don't fit the iambic pattern. You may have remembered me saying that the 5th foot of a pentameter line is never inverted but these lines seem quite clearly to end with MAYK-uhrs and HOP-puhrs, that is with trochees, not iambs.

It's the same story we found with "forefinger." Shakespeare did, in fact, say COACH-may-KUHRS and GRASS-hah-PUHRS. The first few times you try them, it will probably feel and sound awkward and too strange but once you recall that the relatively heavy syllable need only be *somewhat* more emphatic than the relatively light syllable, then you will learn to slide through such words in a way that is both correct and not noticeably odd. Which is very desirable.

These two apparently difficult and troubling lines turn out to be simple, stock lines.

Now let's look at a bit of a speech that is loaded with knotty problems. These are from *Hamlet*, 1.2. King Claudius is speaking to Hamlet before the court. See how many of these lines you can scan before you read my solution.

'Tis sweet and commendable in your nature, Hamlet,	87
To give these mourning duties to your father,	
But you must know your father lost a father,	
That father lost, lost his—and the survivor bound	90
In filial obligation for some term	
To do obsequious sorrow. But to persever	
In obstinate condolement is a course	
Of impious stubbornness, 'tis unmanly grief,	94

But There's a Catch

It doesn't take long to find the first bump, does it? For most, "commendable" is a huge roadblock. I think it takes either a lucky guess or a lot of concordance examination of similar words (or a quick look at the section of this book called "A Special Case of Diddleys: able"). Anyway, the line comes together quickly once you realize that Shakespeare's way was to say <u>KAH</u>-men-DUH-bull, something like "common bubble." All words of that general shape share that rhythm pattern. Check out honorable, hospitable, and comfortable, for example.

Are you ready now to call this a stock line? Or is your tapping so precise that you noticed this line has six and a half feet, not five? Can this happen, legitimately? It does, rarely. Why? It usually takes some masterful interpretive work to answer that question.

In this case, however, something interesting is going on, and it's worth pondering. In the 128 lines of the scene that lead up to Hamlet's soliloquy, Gertrude has one six-footer; Hamlet has none, though he talks plenty; Claudius has six lines of 6 or 6.5 feet. Three of them are explained by Silent Beats in mid-line. Both of those numbers are extreme for such a small scene. They have something to do with the inner turmoil of a king trying to maintain his all's-well front while being publically humiliated by Hamlet.

Lines 88 and 89 seem stock to me.
> To give these mourning duties to your father,
> But you must know your father lost a father,

Both are stock-feminine. You might be tempted to invert "must know" in line 89 or "and the" in line 90 but don't. There's no good reason and they work fine as they stand.

Do you find a problem in 91?
> In filial obligation for some term

I hope so. If you don't, either you aren't counting carefully enough or you have a sensitive intuition for iambic rhythm. If you feel the lump, where does your tap conflict with your spoken rhythm? It should happen at "obli." Back up a syllable or two and start looking for the villain, the word that may have been misspoken. I think you will spot "filial" as the likely culprit. You should recognize it as the kind of word that often gets stretched or shrunken. If your road was bumpy here, try the two-syllable version, FEEL-yuhl, and see how quickly it smoothes out. Tell yourself to remember that the suffix "ial" is almost always compressed, as are all similar suffixes

Line 92 gets really tough.
> To do obsequious sorrow. But to persever

While you're still struggling with an attack from the front, it blindsides you from the middle. You hit a big obstacle when you get to "sor-ROW." You've learned to back up from those obstacles to look for the cause and your find "obsequious" has what looks suspiciously like the kind of compressible suffix you found in the previous line so you try a three-syllable version and, though it doesn't slip off the tongue as sweetly as "filial" did, after a bit of practice it seems obviously right.

So you proceed, and "sorrow" sounds great, and then you almost twist your ankle in the hole left by a missing syllable between "sorrow" and "But." Can you have counted the whole line wrong? No. What does that leave you? Should you have given an extra syllable to some word? Look at them. Very unlikely. Could it be a Silent Beat in Mid-Line? Check the situation. Does this moment deserve a Silent Beat? It must be a concentrated moment of high intensity. What do you find? Yes, it is such a moment. Claudius starts his speech in an artificially cordial mode, almost sweet-talking Hamlet, but at this very moment, he can't sustain it, his temper breaks out and he starts with the insults. Great place for a Silent Beat.

One more possible problem in the line. Did you stumble at the end? Did you wonder how to fit "PER-se-VEER" in? This is one of those language problems that sends you to the concordance, which will show you the seven verse lines in which Shakespeare used the word, always emphasized more strongly on the second syllable. Shakespeare asks us to say "puhr-SEH-vuhr."

Relax; line 93 is stock.

You'll need a rest to get ready for line 94.
> Of impious stubbornness, 'tis unmanly grief, (6 ft.)

Or maybe line 92 prepared you for it. My guess is that you didn't take too long to work out the double whammy of "impious" (compressed suffix and odd emphasis: IHM-pyuss) and another Silent Beat in Mid-Line as Claudius escalates his insults and continues his struggle to keep from blowing his top. And it is one of those six-footers.

OK, you've worked through one of the more complicated speeches in Shakespeare. You see that there is more to scansion that knowing the basic rules of Shakespeare's verse system. It also requires a good deal of information and a lot of creative problem solving.

REMEMBER THE BASIC SCANSION PROCESS:

- Tap out the line, boldly and mechanically not trying to act it or make it meaningful.

- Listen for incongruities, bumps in the road.

- Back up from the incongruity 1 or 2 syllables in search of the possible cause, a word that is too long, short, or mis-emphasized.

- Look for the error, starting with the most likely possibilities, given the kind of word you have.

- Do whatever research is necessary.

- Experiment with possible solutions.

- Make creative decisions.

AND IF YOU DON'T? MASSIVELY RUINED LINES

If a speaker doesn't scan, just follows intuition, which basically means old habits and personal mannerisms, he or she not only speaks prose but, in many cases, sets the words at war with Shakespeare's masterful schemes, substituting crude rhythms for some of the Bards most lyrical and refined.

I believe the most notorious example of a massively abused line is this one from *Romeo and Juliet*:

> O Romeo, Romeo! Wherefore art thou Romeo?　　　　　　　ROM 2.2.33

As you know by now, Romeo is a two syllable name (except for the Last-Word Variation and one mid-line period), though most of those who speak it give it three and I flinch every time they do. Spoken correctly, this line pulsates with Juliet's longing. Spoken with the usual three syllables, it has the rhythm of a child's game song. Juliet's two-syllable name (JOOL-yeht) is abused in the same way (JOO-lee-EHT).

Here are two more lines ruined by the three-syllable Romeo. Scan each of these lines and, when you can speak them appropriately, add the extra syllable to Romeo, and see what an ugly transformation occurs. See how tangible the loss is when we make the unintended move from verse to prose.

> So Romeo would, were he not Romeo called,　(stock)　　ROM 2.2.45
>
> Romeo slew Tybalt. Romeo must not live.　(1st inv.)　　ROM 3.1.181

Consider this next powerful line which is usually stripped of its brilliance by simply reading it "straight," that is without solving the obvious scansion problems. The brilliance of the moment is that not just a word or two but the whole line is intensely onomatopoetic: the rhythm and the texture of the words match and amplify the meaning and feeling of the line. If you speak "stale" with two syllables, miss the elision of "unprofitable," and lose the cascade of "flat and un-prof-," that irresistible rhythm disappears and the line becomes ordinary.

The line:
> How weary, stale, flat and unprofitable   HAM 1.2.133

Usual and incorrect way:
> u – / u – / u – / u u – / u u – /
> How weary, sta-le, flat and unpro-fi-ta-ble

Shakespeare's Way:
> u – / u   – / u – / u –   / u –
> How wea-ry, stale, flat and un-prof' ta-ble

**Shakespeare's plays can be entertaining,
even powerful, when done as prose.**

. . .

**They *will not* be what they *can* be
nor will *you* be what *you might* be,
if they and you are made of prose.**

SURPRISES THAT COMPLICATE SCANSION

You now know the fundamentals of Shakespeare's verse technique. To fully access his power, you need to know the most important differences between his language habits and yours, particularly the ones which influence rhythm: the number of syllables and his choice of emphases. What follows is the most important part of that information, though certainly not all of what would be useful to know.

One more time let me assure you that doing it Shakespeare's way will not make you obscure, old-fashioned, or stiff. Collaborating with the greatest playwright of all time is a smarter strategy than competing with him.

THE MEDIAL VOWEL ELISION: "MID-V"

Shakespeare usually didn't speak the medial vowels (vowels with consonants on both sides). For example, for "battery," he says "BAT-tree," not "BAT-tuh-REE." But you can't count on the texts to reveal this to you. Only scanning will tell you which words are, to us, elided.

Here are a few of the words that Shakespeare usually elides. I have omitted the medial vowels and substituted an apostrophe. Say these aloud. You may find a few of them hard to recognize. Get experimental. Be sure to stick with the lighter and heavier emphases. You'll figure it out.

Shakespeare's Verse: A User's Manual

Abra'am	gath'ring	prop'rer
ad**vent**'rous	glist'ning	pros**p**'rous
barb'rism	**har**b'ring	quarr'lous
batt'ring	im**mod**'rate	ran**c**'rous
blem'shes	im**mod**'rate**ly**	**reg**'lar
blust'rer	im**prov**'dent	ren**d**'ring
brav'ry	in**sep**'rate	rhi**noc**'rous
ca**lam**'ty	in**ter**'gat'ries	**rip**'ning
cer'ments	in**t**'**rrup**ter	**robb**'ry
Cic'ly	in**vet**'rate	**sal**'ry
con**cup**'sci**ble**	ir**res**'lute	**Sal**'sbury
con**fed**'racy	**iv**'ry	**sav**'ry
con**fed**'rate	**lech**'rous	**scan**d'lous
con**qu**'rors	**length**'ning	**scatt**'ring
con**qu**'ring	**lib**'ral	**sev**'ral
dang'rous	**ling**'ring	**sev**'rally
de**liv**'ring	**list**'ning	**sist**'ring
diff'rences	**mag**'cal	**should**'ring
diff'ring	mag**nan**'mous	**sland**'rers
diff'cult	**min**'rals	**sland**'ring
diff'**cul**ty	**mar**v'llous	**slan**'drous
em'rald	**med**'cine	**slaught**'ring
ev'lly	mi**rac**'lous	**slipp**'ry
fav'rite	**mur**m'ring	**spec**'lative
fel'ny	**od**'rous	**strength**'ning
fest'ring	**op**'ning	**ten**'ble
fig'ring	**pal**t'ring	**treach**'rous
flatt'rers	par**tic**'larly	**treas**'nous
flatt'rest	**pest**'ring	**Trip**'li
flick'ring	**plas**t'ring	**us**'rers
fool'ry	**pois**'ner	**utt**'reth
fopp'ry	**pois**'nous	**veh**'mency
fug'tive	pre**post**'rous	**vent**'ring
gard'ner	**pres**'dent	**warr**'nting

Mid-V Exercises

Here are some practice lines for Mid-V elisions. The first twelve lines are all stock masculine.

The time will come that foul sin, **gathering** head (gath'ring)	2H4 3.1.72
So every scope by the **immoderate** use (immod'rate)	MM 1.2.126
My credit now stands on such **slippery** ground, (slipp'ry)	JC 3.1.191
In **ivory** coffers I have stuffed my crowns, (iv'ry)	SHR 2.1.350
O, what a scene of **foolery** have I seen, (fool'ry)	LLL 4.3.161
If I begin the **battery** once again (batt'ry)	H5 3.3.7

The word "battery" provides an example of the kinds of unhelpful spelling you will often find. In the original texts, "battery" appears in eleven verse lines. Four times it is spelled "battery"; seven times it is spelled "batt'ry."

This looks like a pronunciation clue, right? Wrong. It is always spoken with two syllables: BAT-tree. Your only defense against such inconsistency is to scan every line carefully. Don't trust spelling.

On the other hand, the word "taken" which appears in 142 verse lines is spelled "taken" in 58 of those uses and "ta'en" in the other 84. The spelling is completely consistent:

"ta'en" = one syllable (tane) and "taken" = 2 syllables, (TAY-kuhn).

Most published texts retain these spellings. How sweet it would be if it were always that way. But it's not; it's very rare, so:

Scan every line.

Take nothing for granted.

By the way, "ta'en" is an example of what we could call a "**Medial Consonant Elision, a Mid-C,**" the omission of a consonant surrounded by two (or more) vowels. Other examples: our bothersome friends heaven, seven, given. But back to the Mid-Vs:

Your man and you are **marvellous** merry sir. (marv'llous)	COE 4.3.58
His **liberal** eye doth give to every one, (lib'ral,)	H5 4.chorus.44
No **medicine** in the world can do thee good. (med'cine)	HAM 5.2.308
We saw him at the **opening** of his tent. (op'ning)	TC 2.3.84
'Tis **dangerous** when the baser nature comes (dang'rous)	HAM 5.2.60
Lo, she is one of this **confederacy**. (confed'racy)	MND 3.2.192

> **The following lines are stock feminine:**

To be corrupt and **treasonous**.
                          Say not **treasonous**.
                                        (treas'nous)[shared line]   H8 1.1.156a-b

Remorseless, **treacherous, lecherous**, kindless villain.
                                  (treach'rous, lech'rous)   MM 3.2.166

Call him a **slanderous** coward and a villain;   (sland'rous)   R2 1.1.61

What **prisoners** of good sort are taken, uncle?   (pris'ners)   H5 4.8.75

The **poisonous** damp of night disponge upon me,   (pois'nous)   ANT 4.9.13

> Practice these lines until the rhythm feels easy and regular and until the shorter, elided form of the Mid-V words feels natural and clear to you.

SOME WORDS HAVE VARIABLE PRONUNCIATIONS

As you recall, Shakespeare's strategy is to follow the basic iambic form very closely and then to surprise us by calculatedly disregarding the form in a limited number of ways. To get full power from these strategic variations, he must not overuse them. This means he wrote a lot of ten foot, "stock" iambic lines, which called for flexibility and ingenuity in his use of language. He needed a big bag of tricks to make his thoughts fit his system. How did he do it?

- He had a huge vocabulary, which included many variations of the same basic words, giving him a choice that fit his immediate need. For example, if he wanted to speak of rousing from sleep, he could choose from *wake, awaken, awakes, awake, awaketh, wak'd, wak'st, waking, waken, wakened, rise, arise, rouse, rouseth*, and that's just for starters. What a variety of rhythmic and textural options his vocabulary of somewhere between 20,000 and 30,000 words, (depending on how you count) gives him. If your vocabulary is big, writing strict verse is more feasible.

- He also used elision, compression, and contraction to slip his thoughts into the available spaces. If "against" won't fit, he says "'gainst"; if "behavior" is too long, he'll use "'havior." Dorothy Sipe wrote a book, *Shakespeare's Metrics*, full of wonderful detail on the great ingenuity with which Shakespeare stretched or shrank words to honor the iambic form strictly.

- He was clever and he knew the classic languages. They provided the raw material with which he could freely invent new words to meet his needs. The lexicographers used to estimate that he invented an average of 81 new words per script. The number has shrunk a bit recently but even the most conservative estimates are impressive. In Shakespeare's time and place, when grammar school children studied Latin and Greek, such things were possible.

Shakespeare's Verse: A User's Manual

- Above all, he was bold and ingenious in varying the pronunciation of words, both in length and emphasis. If you look very carefully at these words, you'll see that he does this in systematic ways, in ways that make sense and make it easy for the audience to understand them despite the changes.

> Here are pairs of lines to demonstrate variability of pronunciation.
>
> Drill them in order to develop your flexibility.
>
> The key word in the first line of each pair calls for one syllable.
>
> The second line calls for two.

By **heaven**, I'll make a ghost of him that lets me! (1 syl)	HAM 1.4.85
More pious debts to **heav**-en than in all (2 syl)	CYM 3.3.72
Most miserable **hour** that e'er time saw (1)	ROM 4.5.44
'Tis not an **ho**-ur since I left them there. (2)	TIT 2.3.256
Hast thou the **flower** there? Welcome, wanderer. (1)	MND 2.1.247
The field's chief **flow**-er, sweet above compare, (2)	VEN 8
Let's **follow** him, and pervert the present wrath (1)	CYM 2.4.151
And it must **foll**-ow, as the night the day, (2)	HAM 1.3.79
I'll set thee in a **shower** of gold, and hail (1)	ANT 2.5.45
To rain a **sho**-wer of commanded tears, (2)	TS induc 1.123
I'll to the **tower** with all the haste I can (1)	1H6 1.1.167
Hath here distrained the **tow**-er to his use. (2)	1H6 1.3.61

Some Words Have Variable Pronunciations

> **The following pairs vary from two syllables to three.**
> **All of the lines are stock.**

Let me have **au**-dience for a word or two. (2 syl)	AYL 5.4.148
And call the noblest to the **au**-di-**ence**. (3)	HAM 5.2.381
For Christian shame, put by this **bar**-barous brawl. (2)	2H6 4.1.146
O, **bar**-bar-**ous** and bloody spectacle! (3)	OTH 2.3.166
Himself the primrose path of **dal**-liance treads (2)	HAM 1.3.50
My business cannot brook this **dal**-li-**ance**. (3)	COM 4.1.59
The sight of me is **od**-ious in their eyes; (2)	2H6 4.4.46
Which, since they are of you, and **o**-di-**ous** (3)	H8 3.2.331
Why that's my dainty **Ar**-iel! I shall miss thee, (2)	TMP 5.1.95
Fine apparition! My quaint **A**-ri-**el**, (3)	TMP 1.2.317

Notice here some good opportunities for the clarifying technique that helps you work with these shorter forms: the device of moving the final consonant of the shortened word to the beginning of the next word.

"By heaven I'll" becomes "By hehv-nile," which is much easier to say and to hear. This only works when the second word begins with a vowel.

Here are four more:

"follow him" becomes "**fahl**-whim"

"shower of" becomes "**shah**-ruhv"

"heaven unto" becomes "**hehv**-nuhn-too"

"heaven and" becomes "**hehv**-nand"

SOME OTHER VARIABLE WORDS & NAMES

Practice these unfamiliar pronunciations. If you don't, old habits will mislead you at crunch time. The first numbers indicate normal pronunciation; the second, the variant. Practice saying each word aloud at both lengths until both feel natural.

albeit (2/3)	Exeter (2/3)	perdition (3/4)
alien (2/3)	flatterer (2/3)	petition (3/4)
Ariel (2/3)	flattery (2/3)	physician (3/4)
audience (2/3)	fliers (1/2)	pitying (2/3)
Antonio (3/4)	Fulvia (2/3)	promontory (3/4)
authority (4/3)	gardeners (2/3)	promotions (3/4)
Beatrice (2/3)	Glendower (2/3)	propriety (3/4)
briers (2/1)	Gloucester (2/3)	prosperous (2/3)
cardinals (2/3)	Gratiano (3/4)	puissance (3/2)
chariot (2/3)	Helena (2/3)	pyramids (2/3)
charitable (4/3)	Hermia (2/3)	remembrance (3/4)
Charmian (2/3)	higher (2/1)	reverend (2/3)
Claudio (2/3)	hire (1/2)	reverent (2/3)
companion (3/4)	humbler (2/3)	ruinous (2/3)
constitution (4/5)	ignorant (3/2)	Salisbury (3/2)
continuance (3/4)	imitation (4/5)	sanctuary (3/2/4)
contribution (4/5)	inestimable (4/5)	seventy (2/3)
conversation (4/5)	interruption (4/5)	soldiers (2/3)
convocation (4/5)	Juliet (2/3)	suborned (2/3)
deliverance (3/4)	licentious (3/4)	Tamora (3/2)
delivery (3/4)	memories (2/3)	Theseus (2/3)
Demetrius (3/4)	Lewis (1/2)	Tranio (2/3)
diligent (3/2)	Litio (2/3)	treacherous (2/3)
Dromio (2/3)	marrying (2/3)	valiant (2/3)
especial (3/4)	miscarrying (3/4)	vehement (2/3)
Ethiope (2/3)	Parthia (2/3)	villain (1/2)
fiddler (2/3)	particular (3/4)	villainous (2/3)

THE LAST-WORD VARIATION: "L-W VAR"

You are most likely to find a variant pronunciation in the last position in a line. Many words take their longer form only at the end of the line. I call this the Last-Word Variation (aka L-W VAR). Shakespeare uses this device to make the end of the line more important, more obvious. He had many of these consistent habits. The most common kind of L-W VAR words end in IO, IA, ION, IUS, IOUS, UOUS, IAN, IUM, UAL, IENCE, UENCE and similar suffixes. We tend to have a lot of trouble with such words. Shakespeare typically gave these suffixes one syllable and, with a few exceptions, we like to give them two (with the exception of "ion").

Some kinds of words consistently fall into the Last-Word Variation. For example, words ending in **"ION"** or **"IO."** "Petruchio" is properly pronounced peh-**TROOK**-kyoh. When Shakespeare's plan calls for the longer form, we say peh-**TROOK**-kee-**YOH**. The added syllable comes from separating the "i" and the "o" which are normally a diphthong. This is easy for most Americans because our unfortunate inclination is to say "ee-OH" or "ee-AH" always. The appropriate short forms come slower to us.

On the other hand, we find the short "ion" irresistible and the long form very hard. Most of us are a bit frightened by it. When we find "licentious" at the end of a line and we're asked to say lye-**SEN**-chee-**USS**, it can be spooky . . . if you're still stuck with the overly formal Shakespeare image or the got-to-make-him-modern fallacy. But if you take a look at the line this L-W VAR appears in and remember the over-the-top, self-dramatizing, forlorn housewife who says it, in *The Comedy of Errors*, the L-W VAR is the perfect tool to express her excess: Berating her husband, she says "Shouldst thou but hear I were licentious." Milk that L-W VAR fully and you've got a top-ten laugh.

Not all L-W VARs have that intense impact but they all have purpose and punch. If done confidently and subtly, they will not seem artificial. (Lucky British actors. There are still those in Britain whose natural speech includes the stretched ion, making it more familiar and easier to acquire.)

Here are a few examples of Last-Word Variation words. The numbers in parentheses tell how many syllables the word gets when it is in any foot other than the last one in a line, then how many when it is the last. Practice saying this aloud with both syllable counts.

alien	(2/3)	insurrection	(4/5)
companion	(3/4)	invention	(3/4)
conditions	(3/4)	invocation	(4/5)
contemplation	(4/5)	licentious	(3/4)
continuance	(3/4)	passion	(2/3)
Ethiope	(2/3)	patience	(2/3)
function	(2/3)	propriety	(3/4)
Hyperion	(3/4)	protestation	(4/5)
imagination	(5/6)	treacherous	(2/3)
inspiration	(4/5)	usurpation	(4/5)
instigation	(4/5)	vehement	(2/3)
instruction	(3/4)	visitation	(4/5)

Of these words, only "**E**-thiope," "Hy-**per**-ion," and "pro-**prie**-ty" are surprising in their short forms; the others present no problem. After a bit of practice, they begin to feel appropriate. Handle the long form very subtly, very gently. Speak the extra syllable but don't call too much attention to it. Here are some samples of normal and L-W VAR lines for practice:

Some well-trained actors pronounce the two-syllable "tion" "she-**UN**"; some prefer "see-**UN**." I recommend "she-**UN**" because it calls less attention to itself.

But there be new con-**di**-tions, which you'll hear of (3)	TNK 4.1.29
And leave her on such slight con-**di**-ti-**ons**. (4)	TGV 5.4.139
His **con**-tem-**pla**-tion were above the earth (4)	H8 3.2.131
So sweet is zealous **con**-tem-**pla**-ti-**on**. (5)	R3 3.7.93
I can but say their **pro**-tes-**ta**-tion over. (4)	LLL 1.1.33
Here is a coil with **pro**-tes-**ta**-ti-**on**. (5)	TGV 1.2.99

The Last-Word Variation: "L-W Var"

Are you com-**pan**-ion to the Count Ro-**ssill**-ion? (3)   AWW 2.3.192
To have you therein my com-**pan**-i-**on**. (4)   H8 3.2.143

Prove true, i-**mag**-i-**na**-tion, O, prove true (5)   TN 3.4.366
Such tricks hath strong i-**mag**-i-**na**-ti-**on**, (6)   MND 5.1.18

That I should love a bright par-**tic**-'lar star (3)   AWW 1.1.86
(So singular in each par-**tic**-u-**lar**) (4)   WT 4.4.144

You spend your **pas**-sion on a mispriz'd mood. (2)   MND 3.2.74
But till this afternoon his **pas**-si-**on** (3)   COE 5.1.47

Sprinkle cool **pa**-tience. Whereon do you look? (2)   HAM 3.4.125
Drives him beyond the bounds of **pa**-ti-**ence** (3)   1H4 1.3.200

By long and **veh**-'ment suit I was seduc'd (2)   KJ 1.1.254
Their loud applause and Aves **ve**-he-**ment**; (3) Aves=AH-vays   MM 1.1.70

As every **a**-lien pen hath got my use (2)   SON 78
If it be prov'd against an **a**-li-**en** (3)   MV 4.1.345

And the con-**tin**-uance of their parents rage, (3)   ROM Prol, 10
Than my faint means would grant con-**tin**-u-**ance**. (4)   MV 1.1.125

Is a black **Eth**-iope, reaching at the sun. (2)   PER 2.2.20
I'll hold my mind were she an **Eth**-i-**ope**. (3)   ADO 5.4.38

What rein can hold li-**cent**-ious wickedness (3)   H5 3.3.22
Shouldst thou but hear I were li-**cent**-i-**ous**? (4)   COE 2.2.131

From her pro-**pri**-'ty. What's the matter masters? (3)   OTH 2.3.167
That makes thee strangle thy pro-**pri**-e-**ty**. (4)   TN 5.1.145

Most of us are surprised to learn that one syllable is the norm for "io" and "ia" endings. It takes drill to overcome habits and get them rooted. It may take a while to remember to speak them as one syllable but when you do, they sound quite normal. Try mentally translating "io" and ia" to "yo" and "ya." The longer forms are no problem. Here are a few:

Antonio (3/4)	Bellario (3/4)	Cassio (2/3)
Cassius (2/3)	Charmian (2/3)	Claudio (2/3)
Demetrius (3/4)	Dromio (2/3)	Fulvia (2/3)
Glendower (2/3)	Hyperion (3/4)	Litio (2/3)
Parthia (2/3)	Theseus (2/3)	Tranio (2/3)

But then Au-**fid**-ius was within my view. (3)	COR 1.9.85
So your opinion is, Au-**fi**-di-**us**, (4)	COR 1.2.1
No, **Cass**-ius; for the eye sees not itself (2)	JC 1.2.52
I will do so. But look you, **Cas**-si-**us**, (3)	JC 1.2.181
O, **Char**-mian, I will never go from hence. (2)	ANT 4.15.1
What, what, good cheer! Why, how now, **Char**-mi-**an**?(3)	ANT 4.15.82
De-**me**-trius is a worthy gentleman. (3)	MND 1.1.52
If I refuse to wed De-**me**-tri-**us**. (4)	MND 1.1.64
Hy-**per**-ion's curls, the front of Jove himself, (3)	HAM 3.4.56
With entertaining great Hy-**per**-i-**on**. (4)	TRO 2.3.198
My father **Glen**-dower is not ready yet, (2)	1H4 3.1.83
He never did encounter with Glen-**dow**-er. 3)	1H4 1.3.113
His name is **Li**-tio, born in Mantua. (2)	SHR 2.1.60
Mistake no more, I am not **Li**-ti-**o** (3)	SHR 4.2.15
In **Par**-thia did I take the prisoner, (2)	JC 5.3.37
The ne'er-yet-beaten horse of **Par**-thi-**a** (3)	ANT 3.1.33

The Last-Word Variation: "L-W Var"

Wedded with **Thes**-eus all in jollity. (2)   MND 4.1.91
Knowing I know thy love to **Thes**-e-**us**? (3)   MND 2.1.76

Long forms aren't confined to line ends, however. Here are samples of variable words in short forms and with long forms both L-W VAR and Mid-Line. Drill these until they feel like old friends:

The itch of his af-**fec**-tion should not then (3)   ANT 3.13.7
Yet have I fierce af-**fec**-ti-**ons**, and think (4)   ANT 1.5.17
And tender me forsooth af-**fec**-ti-**on**, (4)   MND 3.2.230

O my An-**to**-nio, I do know of these (3)   MV 1.1.95
An-**to**-ni-**o**, my father, is deceas'd, (4)   SHR 1.2.54
You look not well Signior An-**to**-ni-**o**. (4)   MV 1.1.73
Thou blushest, **An**-t'ny, and that blood of thine (2)   ANT 1.1.30
Sir, sometimes, when he is not **An**-to-**ny**, (3)   ANT 1.1.57
Mark **An**-to-**ny**, so well belov'd of Caesar, (3)   JC 2.1.156

Because au-**thor**-'ty, though it err like others, (3)   MM 2.2.134
A man of great au-**tho**-ri-**ty** in France, (4)   1H6 5.1.18
Whereto thy speech serves for au-**tho**-ri-**ty**. (4)   TN 1.2.20

For look where **Bea**-trice, like a lapwing, runs (2)   ADO 3.1.24
There shalt thou find my cousin **Be**-a-**trice** (3)   ADO 3.1.2
Now, Ursula, when **Be**-a-**trice** doth come, (3)   ADO 3.1.15

We will ex-**ten**-uate rather than enforce. (3)   ANT 5.2.125
And so ex-**ten**-u-**ate** the 'forehand sin. (4)   ADO 4.1.48
Which by no means we may ex-**ten**-u-**ate** (4)   MND 1.1.120

Dark night, that from the eye his **func**-tion takes, (2)   MND 3.2.177
That **func**-ti-**on** is smothered in surmise, (3)   MAC 1.3.140
Or what is he of basest **func**-ti-**on** (3)   AYL 2.7.79

Abominable **Glou**-cester, guard thy head, (2)	1H6 1.3.87
Open the gate, 'tis **Glou**-ces-**ter** that calls. (3)	1H6 1.3.4
It is the noble Duke of **Glou**-ces-**ter**. (3)	1H6 1.3.6
Fie, fie, Gra-**tia**-no, where are all the rest? (3)	MV 2.6.62
For **Gra**-ti-**a**-no never lets me speak. (4)	MV 1.1.107
And pardon me, my gentle **Gra**-ti-**a**-no, (4)	MV V.1.260
His folly, **Hel**-'na, is no fault of mine. (2)	MND 1.1.200
And **Hel**-le-**na** of Athens look thou find (3)	MND 3.2.95
Made love to Nedar's daughter, **He**-le-**na**, (3)	MND 1.1.107
What say you, **Herm**-ia? Be advised, fair maid: (2)	MND 1.1.46
Not **Her**-mi-**a** but **Hel**-le-**na** I love. (3)	MND 2.2.119
Where is Lysander and fair **Her**-mi-**a**? (3)	MND 2.1.189
Confound the **ig**-n'rant and amaze indeed (2)	HAM 2.2.565
For I am **ig**-no-**rant** and cannot guess. (3)	1H6 2.5.60
Whereof I know she is not **ig**-no-**rant**. (3)	SHR 2.1.58
Among the **inf**-'nite doings of the world, (2)	WT 1.2.253
Beyond the **in**-fi-**nite** and boundless reach (3)	KJ 4.3.117
Our duty is so rich, so **in**-fi-**nite**, (3)	LLL 5.2.199
Thou hast so wrong'd my **inn**-'cent child and me (2)	ADO 5.1.63
They are as **in**-no-**cent** as grace itself. (3)	AYL 1.3.54
Did I not tell you she was **in**-no-**cent**? (3)	ADO 5.4.1
I am as **per**-emp-**t'ry** as she's proud-minded (3)	SHR 2.1.131
What **per**-emp-**tor**-y eagle-sighted eye (4)	LLL 4.3.224
Yea, mistress, are you so pe-**remp**-to-**ry**? (4)	PER 2.5.74

The Last-Word Variation: "L-W Var"

Of this most wise re-**bel**-lion, thou goest foremost. (3) — COR 1.1.156
In gross re-**bel**-lion and detested treason. (3) — R2 2.3.108
Unthread the rude eye of re-**bel**-li-**on**, (4) — KJ 5.4.11

[TOWARD: length (1 or 2) and emp (1st and 2nd)]
I met in travel **toward** his warlike father (1) — 1H6 4.3.36
Comes **to**-ward Dunsinane. Arm, arm, and out! (2+1st emp) — MAC 5.5.46
Come, sir, to draw to-**ward** an end with you. (2 + 2nd emp) — HAM 3.4.216

And greedily devour the **treach**-'rous bait. (2) — ADO 3.1.28
To think my poverty is **treach**-e-**rous**. (3) — AYL 1.3.61
For such is a friend now! **Treach**-e-**rous** man, (3) — TGV 5.4.63

EXAMPLES: L-W VAR IN CLOSE PROXIMITY

Shakespeare felt so easy with the variability of pronunciation that he often used a second version in very close proximity to a first. Check these samples:

Poor, forlorn Proteus passionate Proteus (2,3)	TGV 1.2.124
The gods make this a happy day to Antony! (2)	ANT 4.5.1
Our will is Antony be took alive; (3)	ANT 4.6.2
Content with Hermia? No, I do repent (2)	
The tedious minutes I with her have spent.	
Not Hermia but Helena I love. (3)	MND 2.2.117-119
Romeo! My cousin Romeo! Romeo! (2,2,3)	ROM 2.1.3.1
Though heaven cannot. X O Romeo, Romeo. (2,2)	
Whoever would have thought it? Romeo! (3)	ROM 3.2.41-42
Hie to your chamber. I'll find Romeo. (3)	ROM 3.2.138
Hark ye, your Romeo will be here at night. (2)	ROM 3.2.140

Develop your rhythmic flexibility and sensitivity by practicing with these lines. You will be ready when the shift from one length to the other comes. It'll come easily and quickly and seem natural and useful.

COMPRESSIONS

In the last section, you saw many "compressions," short form pronunciations of words to which we typically give one more syllable that Shakespeare did. It's not really appropriate to say that he compressed them. The short form is so common in his pronunciation that it must have been to him the "normal" manner of speech and those rare occasions when he used the longer forms should be seen as special, as done for a purpose, and we ought to search for those purposes.

Meanwhile, we need to resist our tendency to slip our modern, long-form pronunciations into his text. They are so automatic for us that it is hard to resist them.

Sensitize yourself to this danger. Scan your lines and alert yourself to the pitfall words.

Try drilling these sample lines with compressions. They're all stock male or female lines except the few noted as "1st inv.". I've made it easy. All these compressed words are names, except for "rapier."

No, Cassius; for the eye sees not itself	JC 1.2.52
'Tis strange, my Theseus, that these lovers speak of.	MND 5.1.1
Help me away, dear Charmian! I shall fall. (1st inv.)	ANT 1.3.15
Gentle Mercutio, put thy rapier up. (1st inv.) (Mercutio *and* rapier)	ROM 3.1.82
I pray you, good Bassanio, let me know it,	MV 1.1.135
Gremio, 'tis now no time to vent our love. (1st inv.)	SHR 1.2.176
And therefore, Tranio, for the time I study	SHR 1.1.17
I can, Petruchio, help thee to a wife	SHR 1.2.84

Rise, Grumio, rise. We will compound this quarrel.	SHR 1.2.27
There, there, Hortensio, will you any wife?	SHR 1.1.56
Alas, Malvolio, this is not my writing,	TN 5.1.343
Be thou assured, good Cassio, I will do	OTH 3.3.1
And so she shall. Lucentio shall make one,	SHR 1.2.243
From both, my lord. Bellario greets your grace	MV 4.1.120
Now, daughter Silvia, you are hard beset.	TGV 2.4.47
Put forth toward Phrygia, and their vow is made	TC prologue.7
Came you from Padua, from Bel-**lar**-i-**o**? (L-W VAR)	MV 4.1.119
Hamlet in madness hath Polonius slain, (1st inv.)	HAM 4.1.34
And moody Pluto winks while Orpheus plays.	LUC 553
Sweet Proteus, no; now let us take our leave.	TGV 1.1.56
Than is Prometheus tied to Caucasus.	TIT 2.1.17
What say you, Hermia? Be advised, fair maid;	MND 1.1.46
Come with a thought. I thank thee, Ariel. Come! (1st inv.)	TEM 4.1.164

"EVEN," "E'EN," and "E'VN"

There are three forms of the word "even": even, e'en, and e'vn. In almost every appearance, they are best pronounced the same way: one syllable "een."

The printing of the texts is erratic on this matter. You can't rely on either the original texts or the newly edited ones to reveal whether the word gets one or two syllables. **You must scan each line to find out.**

When they are one syllable, I recommend pronouncing them EEN, simply, crisply. Don't try to crowd in a remnant of the "uhn."

E'EN: All of the verse uses of "E'EN" in the original texts are **one syllable**. Here are some samples of verse lines with "e'en":

Is it e'en so? Why then I thank you all.	ROM 1.5.123
Is it e'en so? Then I defy you stars!	ROM 5.1.24
I think it be no other but e'en so.	HAM 1.1.108
Horatio, thou art e'en as just a man	HAM 3.2.64
Will e'en but kiss Octavia, and we'll follow.	ANT 2.4.3
No more but e'en a woman and commanded	ANT 4.15.72
Than such that do e'en enemies exceed.	TIM 1.2.203
And e'en as if your lord should wear rich jewels	TIM 3.4.25

(There are also 23 prose uses which, we may assume, ought to be pronounced as one syllable.)

> All 17 of the verse uses of "Ev'n" are one syllable except for the one use in which the word means "evening."
>
> In that one case, it gets two syllables:
> *Madam, good ev'n to your ladyship.*   TGV 4.2.85

EV'N:

And ev'n that power which gave me first my oath	TGV 2.6.4
And ev'n in kind love I do conjure thee,	TGV 2.7.2
Why, ev'n that fashion thou best likes, Lucetta.	TGV 2.7.52
O grandsire, grandsire, ev'n with all my heart	TIT 5.3.171
I am mightily abus'd; I should ev'n die with pity (I am = I'm; 6½ ft.)	KL 4.7.53
Which must be ev'n as swiftly followed as	WT 1.2.409
Mine eyes, ev'n sociable to the show of thine (sociable = SOHSH-buhl)	TEM 5.1.63
You must ev'n take it patiently.	TNK 4.1.115.1
'Tis true. (shared line)	TNK 4.1.115.2
Ev'n when you will.	TNK 5.2.85.1
O, sir, you'ld fain be nibbling. (shared line)	TNK 5.2.85.2
I must ev'n leave you here.	TNK 5.2.100.1
Nay, we'll go with you. (shared line)	TNK 5.2.100.2
Ev'n he that led you to this banquet shall	TNK 5.4.22
In this place first you fought; ev'n very here	TNK 5.4.99
Ev'n in this thought through the dark night he stealeth, (3rd foot inv.)	LUC.729

"EVEN", "E'EN", and "E'VN"

> For the three of these lines in which "ev'n" is followed by a word beginning with a vowel, it is best to say "EEV" instead of "EEN." Example: speak "Ev'n in" as "eev nin"; this sound is a bit more familiar to the audience and just as rhythmically correct.

EVEN:

The spelling **"even"** appears 629 times in Shakespeare's works. It is usually a one syllable word but there are several at two syllables. Here are samples:

ONE SYLLABLE (speak them "een")

Even now, even here, not half an hour since	COE 2.2.14
Villain, thou liest, for even her very words	COE 2.2.172
Even in the spring of love, thy love-springs rot?	COE 3.2.3
She that doth call me husband, even my soul	COE 3.2.166
Even just the sum that I do owe to you	COE 4.1.7
Come, come, you know I gave it you even now	COE 4.1.55
Even now a tailor call'd me in his shop,	COE 4.3.7
Even now we housed him in the abbey here,	COE 5.1.188
Even for the service that long since I did thee,	COE 5.1.191
Deep scars to save thy life; even for the blood	COE 5.1.193
Even in the strength and height of injury:	COE 5.1.200
Even as a flatt'ring dream or worthless fancy.	SHR induction.1.42

TWO SYLLABLES:

And the moon changes even as your mind.	SHR 4.5.20
Losing his verdure, even in the prime,	TG 1.1.49
Hast thou observ'd that? Even she I mean.	TG 2.1.42
You have your wish: my will is even this,	TG 4.2.90
I do desire thee, even from a heart	TG 4.3.32
Were not you here but even now, disguis'd?	LLL 5.2.433
Will even weigh; and both as light as tales.	MND 3.2.133

WORDS ENDING IN "EST" AND "'ST"

> **RULE OF THUMB:**
>
> For most of these words it is inappropriate to pronounce the "est" or "'st" as a separate syllable. This is almost always true for verbs (which most of these words are) and for many of the adjectives.

HERE ARE EXAMPLES FOR DRILL: These words are almost randomly spelled "est" or " 'st" in the original texts. You can't depend on the difference in any old or new text to tell you pronunciation. The only way to find out is to scan each line. For regularity and to make the words more recognizable, I have spelled all with an "est" here. When creating a performance script, I use the "est" and " 'st" consistently to indicate pronunciation.

ONE-SYLLABLE VERBS:

camest	sentest	pluckest	saidest
showest	seest	sitest	taughtest
cutest	scaldest	walkest	speakest
foughtest	pryest	wearest	splitest
knowest	barest	copest	stayest
huntest	beest	criedest	diedest
fearest	bleedest	diest	prunest
hangest	dippedest	keepest	runest
strewest	fellest	lovedest	damnest
talkest	feltest	feelest	
sendest	notest	bearest	

TWO-SYLLABLE VERBS:

consumest	preventest	restrainest	buriest
deniest	contrivedest	perceivest	usurpest
flatterest	esteemest	commitest	pursuest
pitiedest	presentest	wholesomest	

SOME OF THE FEW "EST" VERBS WHICH ARE NOT "COMPRESSED":

They aren't compressed because the sound of the root word doesn't allow for an easy contraction. Try to compress them and you'll see what I mean.

vanishest	(3 syllables)
diffusest	(3 syllables)
usest	(2 syllables)

NON-COMPRESSED ADJECTIVES:

basest	fiercest	rudest
eftest	furthest	strictest
eldest	hottest	surest
exactest	justest	vilest
fewest	roughest	

COMPRESSED ADJECTIVES:
(all 2 syllables)

bitterest	daintiest	lustiest
bloodiest	damned'st	proudest
chariest	humblest	speediest
cursedst	loyall'st	weariest

Words Ending in "EST" and "'ST"

COMPRESSED SUFFIXES:

We are used to pronouncing most suffixes with one more syllable than Shakespeare wants. To him, the short form was the norm. To us, these seem like compressions. Here are some of them with a couple of examples.
All of them are normally spoken as one syllable.

When these appear as the last word in a verse line, they are likely to be Last-Word Variations. (The numbers in () show the appropriate number of syllables.)

IATE: immediate (ih-MEE-djuht) (3)

IUM: Antium (AN- tyuhm) (2), Epidamnium (4)

IOUS: incestuous (in-SEHSS-chwuhss (3), sumptuous (2), ambiguous (3), voluptuousness (vuh-LUP-chwuss-NESS) (4)

UING: issuing (ISH-wing) (2)

IAL: material (muh-TEER-yuhl) (3), memorial (3), filial (2)

UAL: annual (AN-yuhl) (2), continually (3), effectually (ee-FEHK-chwuh-LEE)

IO and **IA** (**yoh** and **yah** or **yuh** as in Peh-TROO-kyoh and GROOM-yoh); found in almost every Italian name and more.

IANT: radiant (RAY-dyuhnt) (2)

IEST: speediest (SPEE-dyuhst) (2), lustiest (2)

IAN: ruffian (RUH-fyuhn) (2)

YING and **LING**: tarrying (TARE-ying) (2), ruffling (RUFF-ling) (2), jangling (2), justifying (3), marrying (2)

UAL: sensual (SEHN-shwuhl) (2), spiritual (SPEER-chwuhl) (2)

―――――― Shakespeare's Verse: A User's Manual ――――――

Here are a few sentences including words with compressed suffixes. Play with them until you get the habit.

No, **Cas**sius; for the eye sees not itself	JC 1.2.52
'Tis strange, my **Thes**eus, that these lovers speak of.	MND 5.1.1
Help me away, dear **Char**mian! I shall fall.	ANT 1.3.15
Gentle Mer**cu**tio, put thy rapier up.	ROM 3.1.82
I pray you, good Bas**san**io, let me know it,	MV 1.1.135
Gremio, 'tis now no time to vent our love.	SHR 1.2.176
And therefore, **Tra**nio, for the time I study	SHR 1.1.17
I can, Pe**truch**io, help thee to a wife	SHR 1.2.84
Rise, **Grum**io, rise. We will compound this quarrel.	SHR 1.2.27
There, there, Hor**tens**io, will you any wife?	SHR 1.1.56
Alas, Mal**vol**io, this is not my writing,	TN 5.1.343
Be thou assured, good **Cas**sio, I will do	OTH 3.3.1
And so she shall. Lu**cen**tio shall make one,	SHR 1.2.243
From both, my lord. Bel**lar**io greets your grace	MV 4.1.120
Now, daughter **Sil**via, you are hard beset.	TGV 2.4.47
Put forth toward **Phry**gia, and their vow is made	TC prologue.7
Came you from **Pa**dua, from Bellario?	MV 4.1.119
Hamlet in madness hath Po**lon**ius slain,	HAM 4.1.34
And moody Pluto winks while **Or**pheus plays.	LUC.553
Than is Pro**meth**eus tied to **Cauca**sus.	TIT 2.1.17

"ODD-EMPS": WORDS WITH UNEXPECTED EMPHASES

Many of Shakespeare's words are emphasized on different syllables than we emphasize. We must use his emphasis or we will undermine his verse rhythms. Here are a few samples. The **bold** syllable receives the greater emphasis.

acces**so**ry	con**vertite**	**mul**ber**ry**
ances**try**	cur**tailed**	op**por**tune
ar**tif**i**cer**	**dam**ask	out**right**
as**pect**	dic**ta**tor	Phil**li**pi
Barra**bas**	di**late**	Pos**thu**mous
Bartol'**mew**	else**where**	**Pu**celle
Burdeaux	es**quire**	**pur**vey**or**
Campa**ne**us	Fitz**wa**ter	**quin**tes**sence**
cannot	hu**mane**	re**cord**
ca**non**iz'd	Her**cu**lean	re**flex**
char**ac**ter'd	il**lus**tra**ted**	Semi**ra**mis
cha**rac**te**ry**	**im**pious	se**pul**chring
comba**tant**	in**stinct**	**se**quest'**ring**
commen**da**ble	**in**to	spec**ta**tors
confine	**Lan**caster	sub**se**quent
contents (vb. & noun)	leave-**tak**ing	**su**preme
con**trac**ted	**ma**chine	sur**named**
contrary	**Mil**an	**tra**vail
conver**sant**	mis**con**strued	**Val**entius

Lack of this kind of historical information is one of the most subversive underminers of classical actors. Even those who try diligently to scan their lines are likely to boggle when they come to such odd problems as some of the words given above present. And there are many more, just as unexpected.

Shakespeare's Verse: A User's Manual

Fortunately, three useful pronouncing dictionaries have been published in the last few years. Use them! They are Dale Coye's *Pronouncing Shakespeare's Words*; Louis Scheeder and Shane Ann Younts' *All the Words on Stage*; and Gary Logan's *The Eloquent Shakespeare*.

Work with these lines until the unexpected words feel normal to you.

Another lean unwash'd ar**tificer**	KJ 4.2.201
Caesar and **Ant**'ny shall well greet together.	ANT 2.1.39
Come with a thought. I thank thee, **Ariel**. Come!	TEM 4.1.164
Would any of the stock of **Bar**rabas	MV 4.1.293
Sirrah, go you to **Bar**thol'mew my page,	SHR ind.1.103
For look where **Bea**trice, like a lapwing, runs	ADO 3.1.24
To **Bor**deaux, warlike Duke! To **Bor**deaux, York!	1H6 4.3.22
Tell you the **Dau**phin, I am coming on,	H5 1.2.292
Now, **Dian**, from thy altar do I fly,	AWW 2.3.73
Fitz**wa**ter, thou art damned to hell for this.	R2 4.1.43
Why did he marry **Ful**via, and not love her?	ANT 1.1.41
I'll steal to **Glen**dower, and Lord Mortimer,	1H4 1.3.289
His folly, **Hel**'na, is no fault of mine.	MND 1.1.200
What say you, **Her**mia? Be advis'd, fair maid;	MND 1.1.46
The Duke of **Lan**caster and **West**morland;	2H4 1.3.82
Her name is **Ka**the**ri**na **Mi**nola,	SHR 1.2.98
And set the murderous **Mach**iavel to school.	3H6 3.2.193
O sweet Ma**ri**a, empress of my love! –	LLL 4.3.54
O **Pan**darus! I tell thee, **Pan**darus –	TC 1.1.49

"Odd-Emps": Words with Unexpected Emphases

That I am **Pros**-p'ro, and that very Duke	TEM 5.1.159
What, **Pin**darus! Where art thou, **Pin**darus?	JC 5.3.72
I did not think to draw my sword 'gainst **Pom**pey,	ANT 2.2.159
Where is Pos**thum**us? What is in thy mind	CYM 3.4.4
Sweet **Pro**teus, no; now let us take our leave.	TGV 1.1.56
And to that youth he calls his '**Rosalind**'	AYL 4.3.93
To their sub**se**quent volumes, there is seen	TC 1.3.344
The Earl of **West**morland set forth today,	1H4 3.2.170
When Goths were Goths, and **Tam**ora was queen –	TIT 1.1.143
My Lord of **West**minster, be it your charge	R2 4.1.152
Here, **Win**chester, I offer thee my hand.	1H6 3.1.127
And for our eyes do hate the dire as**pect**	R2 1.3.127
But taking note of thy upti'd as**pect**,	KJ 4.2.224
And afterward con**sort** you till bed**time**.	COE 1.2.28
Between our after-supper and bed**time**?	MND 5.1.34
Ambition **can**not pierce a wink beyond,	TMP 2.1.242
I **can**not leave to love, and yet I do	TGV 2.6.17
May pierce the head of the great **com**ba**tant**.	TC 4.5.5
Come hither, you that would be **com**ba**tants**.	1H6 4.1.134
It stands as an e**dict** in destiny.	MND 1.1.151
Our late e**dict** shall strongly stand in force:	LLL 1.1.11

Of **im**pious stubbornness. **X** Tis unmanly grief. (6 ft.)	HAM 1.2.94
O **im**pious act including all foul harms!	LUC 199
Im**por**tune him once more to go, my Lord	KL 3.4.158
As time and our concernings shall im**por**tune,	MM 1.1.56
By a divine in**stinct** man's mind mistrusts	R3 2.3.42
And mere in**stin**ct of love and loyalty,	2H6 3.2.250
Strong-fixed is the house of **Lan**caster,	1H6 2.5.102
With him my son, Lord John of **Lan**caster,	1H4 3.2.171
Was **Mi**lan thrust from **Mi**lan that his issue	TMP 5.1.233
The gates of **Mi**lan; and in depths of darkness	TMP 1.2.126
And let us not be dainty of leave-**tak**ing,	MAC 2.3.141
Puts back leave-**tak**ing, jostles roughly by	TC 4.4.33
Now humble as the ripest **mul**berry,	COR 3.2.79
With purple grapes, green figs, and **mul**berries.	MND 3.1.162
'Tis ten to one it maimed you two out**right**.	TS 5.2.62
Ah, Joan, this kills thy father's heart out**right**.	1H6 5.4.2
To throw a **per**fume on the violet,	KJ 4.2.12
As made the things more rich. Their **per**fume lost,	HAM 3.1.99
The Dauphin, with one Joan la **Pu**celle joined	1H6 1.4.101
Excellent **Pu**celle, if thy name be so,	1H6 1.2.110

"HEAVEN": A GREAT PLACE BUT A HARD WORD (WITH DIFFICULT FRIENDS)

Here are some samples of the one-syllable "heaven." These are easy. Each can be elided with the word which follows:

From my cold heart let heaven engender hail (HEHV-nehn-JEHN-der)	ANT 3.13.159
'Call me not fool, till heaven hath sent me fortune.' (HEHV-nath)	AYL 2.7.19
That heaven had made her such a man. She thanked me (HEHV-nad)	OTH 1.3.162
Nor heaven nor earth have been at peace tonight. (HEHV-nor)	JC 2.2.1
Smile, heaven, upon this fair conjunction, (HEHV-nuh-PAWN)	R3 5.5.20
As, and't please heaven, he shall not – they should find (HEHV-nee)	MAC 3.6.19
That heaven and earth may strike their sounds (HEHV-nand)	ANT 4.8.38
Comfort's in heaven, and we are on the earth, (HEHV-nand)	R2 2.2.78
The breast of heaven, I did present myself (HEHV-nye)	JC 1.3.51
By heaven I rather would have been his hangman. (HEHV-nye)	OTH 1.1.34
By heaven I would most gladly have forgot it. (HEHV-nye)	OTH 4.1.19
Derives from heaven his quarrel and his cause. (HEHV-nihz)	2H4 1.1.206
That when the searching eye of heaven is hid (HEHV-nihz)	R2 3.2.37
Heaven is my judge, not I for love and duty, (HEHV-nihz)	OTH 1.1.60
By heaven, I'll hate him everlastingly (HEHV-nile)	R2 3.2.207
Who sets me else? By heaven, I'll throw at all! (HEHV-nile)	R2 3.2.207
Heaven and Our Lady gracious hath it pleased (HEHV-nand)	1H6 1.2.74

These are difficult because they cannot be elided. For these, we must learn to pronounce "heaven" as one syllable:

The cannons to the heavens, the heavens to earth,	HAM 5.2.274
Let heaven requite it with the serpent's curse,	OTH 4.2.16
O heaven, that such companions thou'ldst unfold,	OTH 4.2.143
And thank heaven, fasting, for a good man's love.	AYL 3.5.58
Heaven make thee free of it. I follow thee.	HAM 5.2.337
My comfort is, that heaven will take our souls,	R2 3.1.33
Weak men must fall, for heaven still guards the right.	R2 3.2.62
The king of heaven forbid our lord the king	R2 3.3.101
If not to heaven, then hand in hand to hell!	R3 5.3.314
Nor heaven peep through the blanket of the dark,	MAC 1.5.53
Which is too nigh your person. Heaven preserve you!	MAC 4.2.71
Doth glance from heaven to earth, from earth to heaven;	MND 5.1.13
If she be false, O then heaven mocks itself,	OTH 3.3.282

ALL SIMILAR WORDS FOLLOW THIS PATTERN. (E.G., GIVEN, SEVEN, ELEVEN)

The seven-fold shield of Ajax cannot keep	ANT 4.14.38
O heat, dry up my brains. Tears seven-times salt	HAM 4.5.154
Upon the platform twixt eleven and twelve (eh-LEHV-nand)	HAM 1.2.252
That teacheth tricks eleven and twenty long, (eh-LEHV-nand)	SHR 4.2.57
Like poison given to work a great time after.	TMP 3.3.105

THE HARDEST WORD IS THE ONE-SYLLABLE "DEVIL" (BUT EASY WHEN ELIDED):

Thee, and the devil alike. What ho Pisanio! (DEH-vluh-LYKE)	CYM 1.7.14
Nay, if the devil hath given thee proofs for sin, (double hard!)	MM 3.2.29
May be a devil and the devil hath power (1ˢᵗ `2; 2ⁿᵈ `1)	HAM 2.2.595

UNFAMILIAR WORD PRONUNCIATIONS

Here is a small bundle of unusual kinds of pronunciation problem you will find in Shakespeare's verse.

When " **th'** " (meaning "the") appears before a word, it should not be pronounced as a separate syllable. Speak it as a consonant that begins the syllable:

th'encounter = then-COUN-tuhr

th'offender = thuh-FEHN-dehr

th'expanse = thex-PANSE

th'hand = THAND

If you have developed a higher level of skill, you might more effectively add an unvoiced "y" sound to the ("**th'** ") plus the appropriate vowel. For example: thyen-COUN-tuhr. It is harder when the word after the **th'** begins with a consonant. In these cases, the "th'" sound is no more than a brief release of air between the tongue and the upper teeth, with no vowel sounded. It takes some tongue and lip agility but it is important to squeeze all of the necessary sounds into the space. "Th'" becomes just a small hesitation and hiss at the start of the word. Place the tip of your tongue behind your upper teeth and begin your breath before pronouncing the word.

Th'purpose = THPUHR-puhss

th'gods, th'law, th'brains, th'top = one syllable each

Sometimes you will find **o'th'** before a word. It means "of the" and it only gets one syllable (roughly = uth):

o'th'best = uh-THBEHST

o'th'cliff = uh-THCLIHF

o'th'enemy = uh-THEH-nuh-MEE (or uh-THEN-mee)

Sometimes you will find " **I'th'** " before a word, meaning "in the." Treat it as you did o'th':

I'th'cage = ih-THCAGE

I'th'stocks = ih-THSTAHX

I'th'last = ih-THLAST

I'th'imminent = ih-THIM-NENT

Here are some words or terms pronounced more briefly than we usually do:

do't (meaning "do it") = doot

to't (meaning "to it") = toot

being = beeng (usually)

be it = beet (often)

taken or **ta'en** = tane (usually)

fallen = fahln (usually)

power = one syllable; easy to say; almost but not quite = PAR

All "ower" words are like this one. Examples: flower, tower, shower.

Stolen or stol'n = STOHLN

put't ("put it") = one syllable, almost like PUT without the extra 't

may't ("may it") = MATE

upon's ("upon his") = uh-PONZ

carry it (When this is elided, say CARE-yit)

These are just samples of the many differences you will find between Shakespeare's language and ours. They will help you to scan your lines.

**These unfamiliar
pronunciations will sound and
feel odd to you at first.**

**After practice, they will feel not
just normal but very good.**

**Your lines will flow easily
and be more audible
and more vital when you do it
Shakespeare's way.**

A FEW UNFAMILIAR NAME PRONUNCIATIONS

Many of Shakespeare's names are unfamiliar or look familiar but are not pronounced as we think they should be. We can learn a lot by scanning them carefully and by studying Shakespeare's rhymes. Here are some names, all from *Romeo and Juliet* with their pronunciations. I have only included those which didn't seem obvious to me.

Let's start with the two most abused names in all of Shakespeare:

Romeo	= ROHM-yo
Juliet	= JOOL-yuht
Benvolio	= ben-VOHL-yo
Mercutio	= muhr-CUE-shoh
Montague	= MAHN-tuh-GHYU
Capulet	= CAP-yoo-LEHT
Rosaline	= ROSE-uh-LYNE
Tybalt	= TIH-buhlt

Some of these names also have a longer form which is used when they appear at the end of a verse line. These are examples of Shakespeare's **Last-word Variation** which is his way of giving a stronger ending to the verse line, making us *feel* the end more. Pick up on this cue. Make the music of your speech do the same thing the pronunciation is doing.

As usual, the number of syllables is in () with the relatively stronger emphasis in **bold**.

Antony (2 usually; 3)
Ariel (2, in 15 of 19 uses)
Bell**a**rio (3,4)
Barthol'**mew** (3)
Bas**san**io (3)
Beatrice (2 usually; 3)
Be**rowne** (2)

Burdeaux (2)
Cassio (2, 3)
Cassius (2)
Charmian (2)
De**me**trius (3)
Dian (2)
Dromio (2)

Fitz**wa**ter (3)
Fulvia (2)
Glendower (2)
Gremio (2)
Grumio (2)
Helena (50% @ 2)
Ho**ra**tio (3)
Hor**ten**sio (3)
Juliet (2)
Kate (1; = cat)
Katrin (2)
Ka**tri**na (3)
Kate**ri**na (4)
Lancas**ter** (3)
Lor**raine** (2)
Lu**cen**tio (3)
Lucrece (2)
Machiavel (3)
Mal**vo**lio (3)
Mer**cu**tio (3)
Mi**no**la (3)
O**li**via (3)

Orpheus (2)
Padua (2)
Pandarus (3)
Perdita (3)
Pe**truch**io (3)
Phrygia (2)
Pindarus (3)
Po**lon**ius (3)
Post**hu**mous (3)
Pro**meth**eus (3)
Prospero (2, @ 44%)
Proteus (2)
Romeo (2)
Se**mir**amis (4)
Sylvia (2)
Tamora (3)
Theseus (2 @ 50%)
Tranio (2)
Westmore**land** (3)
Westmin**ster** (3)
Winches**ter** (3)

Beware these particularly surprising pronunciations:

Barkloughly (bark-**LOW**-lee)
Barrabas (**BARE**-uh-**BUSS**)
Barthol'mew (**BAR**-tol-MYOO)
Berowne (buh-**ROON**)
Dauphin (**DAW**-fin)

Lewis (loose)
Maria (muh-**RYE**-uh)
Milan (**MILL**-uhn)
Rosalind (**ROSE**-uh-LYND)
Vaughn (**VAW**-kuhn)

Unfamiliar Word Pronunciations

Drill these names in context; check yourself on pages 108 and 109

This goddess, this Semiramis, this nymph.	TIT 2.1.22
It is the east and Juliet is the sun!	ROM 2.2.3
O Romeo, Romeo, wherefore art thou Romeo.	ROM 2.2.33
Is counted lost forever, Perdita,	WT 3.3.27
O when my eyes did see Olivia first,	TN 1.1.19
Come Grey, come Vaughn, let us here embrace. (**VAW**-kuhn)	R3 3.3.25
De**me**trius is a worthy gentleman.	MND 1.1.25
King Lewis and Lady Bona, hear me speak	3H6 3.3.65
Is daughter to the famous Duke of Milan	TMP 5.1.192
Well sit you out, go home Berowne. Adieu!	LLL 1.1.110
And stay there Dromio, till I come for thee;	COE 1.2.10

Some odd-emp words are odd only part of the time and you must rely on your scansion skills to know which hat they're wearing at each moment.
For example:

That thou, dead corse, again in **com**plete steel,	HAM 1.4.52
And now my hope is full, my joy com**plete**:	E3 3.1.53
Of great re**ve**nue; and she hath no child.	MND 1.1.158
The reve**nue** whereof shall furnish us	R2 1.4.46

UNSPOKEN POSSESSIVES

We have seen several of the ways Shakespeare's verse rhythm can be undermined. Most often we do it by adding syllables or by emphasizing a different syllable than he did. The causes of some of these, such as the odd-emp words, obey no clear rule. Others, the Mid-V, for example, are common enough to become pretty obvious once we get the idea and a little practice. We learn to spot them quickly enough. Fortunately, some follow consistent rules, such as the one that governs **"Unspoken Possessives."**

There is a large group of words ending in "s" which, when they become possessive, when they are followed by an apostrophe, we speak with an extra syllable, a "sehz" or "suhz" sound. If you were reading about my last book, you would probably see "Gross' book" and say "GROHS-sehz book." You would read "witness' " and say "WIT-nehs-SEHZ." "Douglas'" would produce "DUHG-luhs-SEZH."

Shakespeare didn't do it that way. He didn't add that extra "SEHZ."

Here is a line from *A Midsummer Night's Dream*:

> Per**haps** till **af**ter **The**seus' **wed**ding **day**.   MND 2.1.139

There are two pitfalls here. First we must avoid adding the unwanted possessive "sehz". Then we must remember that Theseus is a variable name, usually compressed to two syllables. This is a stock line and a very nice one, if you say THEES-yuhss. If you fall into those two pitfalls; adding those two unwanted syllables, it turns to ugly prose: THEE-see-UH-sehz.

Here are two more double-pitfall lines with compressed names as the complicating factor:

> De**serve** a **sweet** look **from** De**me**trius' **eye**,   MND 2.2.133

Unspoken Possessives

The "trius" of Demetrius is, for most of us, a tough compression but careful scansion makes it very clear that it is required and a bit of drill drives out that strange feeling. The coming together of the unfamiliar compression with the unspoken possessive does make this line feel a bit alien at first contact; but not as alien as the sound you get without the compression and with the unwanted "sehz."

Here's the third:

> He'll **beat** Aufidius' **head** be**low** his **knee**   COR 1.3.47

In all of Shakespeare, I find only two words that Shakespeare chose to add the extra "sehz" to: mistress and Mars and in both cases, he pointed out the special pronunciation by adding "'s" after the final "s."

> On **Mars**'s ar**mour**, **forged** for **proof** e**terne**,   HAM 2.2.488

There are five of these 2-syllable "Mars's" and no 1-syllable "Mars'."
There are 36 2-syllable "mistress'" in verse and one lonely 3-syllable "mistress's."

> Ay, **ay**: O, **lay** me **by** my **mis**tress' **side**. (2 syllable)   OTH 5.2.235
> A **mis**tress's com**mand**. Wear **this**; spare **speech**. (3 syllable)   KL 4.2.21

All of these examples are stock, masculine lines.

This is about as close as you get to an absolute rule of pronunciation: words ending in "s" followed by an apostrophe should be spoken just like the same word without the apostrophe.

Here are several sample lines with unspoken possessives. Practice them until it feels natural not to add the dreaded "sehz" when you see an apostrophe floating at the end of a word.

If you pay attention to the contractions and compressions, you'll find that this group of lines, too, is all stock. I'm still taking it easy on you, trying to get that basic rhythm deeply burned into your nervous system.

Full **thir**ty **time**s hath **Phoe**bus' **cart** gone **round**	HAM 3.2.164
In **Saturninus**' **health**, whom, **if** he **sleep**,	TIT 4.4.24
See, **see**, thou hast **shot** off **one** of **Taurus**' **horns**. (thou'st)	TIT 4.3.69
At **Corio**lanus' **exile**. Now he's **com**ing	COR 4.6.134
O **ten** times **fas**ter **Venus**' **pig**eons **fly**	MV 2.6.5
Thy **huntress**' **name** that **my** full **life** doth **sway**.	AYL 3.2.4
And **do** sub**mit** me **to** your **high**ness' **mer**cy.	H5 2.2.77
Hang**ing** the **head** at **Ceres**' **plen**teous **load**? (1st inv.)	2H6 1.2.2
I **got** this **ring**; 'twas **Leona**tus' **jew**el,	CYM 5.5.143
For **Bru**tus' **sake**, I **am** be**hold**ing **to** you.	JC 3.2.66
Look, **in** this **place** ran **Cassius**' **dag**ger **through**;	JC 3.2.175
Thersites' **bo**dy **is** as **good** as **A**jax',	CYM 4.2.252

This list includes most of the words and names that follow this rule. When you see them, resist the temptation to add that modern "sehz." You'll save a lot of beautiful lines from accidental prosing:

A**chi**lles'	Dio**me**des'	Lu**ci**lius'	Po**lo**nius'
A**do**nis'	**Doug**las'	**Mar**tius'	**prin**cess'
An**chi**ses'	**Duch**ess'	Me**ne**laus'	**Pro**teus'
An**dro**nicus'	**Em**press'	**Mu**tius'	**Pyr**rhus'
An**to**nius'	**Fla**vius'	**Ni**lus'	Sat**ur**ninus'
Bas**sia**nus'	**Fu**ries'	Oc**ta**vius'	**So**crates'
Calchas'	**great**ness'	O**lym**pus'	**Tel**lus'
Cocytus'	**Greeks**'	**Or**pheus'	**Te**reus'
Co**mi**nius'	**Has**tings'	**Par**is'	Ti**ti**nius'
Colchos'	**host**ess'	**Pat**roclus'	**The**tis'
Crassus'	**Jew**ess'	**Per**seus'	**Tul**lus'
Cyclops'	**Laer**tes'	**Phoe**bus'	

"MANY A"

This phrase is one of the most consistently elided in all Shakespeare. It also displays one of the most consistent patterns of variation I have found.

In most uses, "many a" is spoken as two syllables: MEHN-yuh, as in these examples:

In high-borne words, the worth of many a knight	LLL 1.1.170
They say that they have measur'd many a mile	LLL 5.2.186
Signior Antonio, many a time and oft	MV 1.3.103
You have among you many a purchas'd slave,	MV 4.1.90
Since many a wooer doth commence his suit	ADO 2.3.48
Who after me hath many a weary step	AYL 2.7.131
Ah, sir, there's many a Greek and Trojan dead	TC 4.5.214
For thou exists on many a thousand grains	MM 3.1.20
Whereto I have invited many a guest,	ROM 1.2.21
Knew you not Pompey? Many a time and oft	JC 1.1.37
How does your honor for this many a day?	HAM 3.1.91
There's many a beast then in a pop'lous city,	OTH 4.1.63
Hath widowed and unchilded many a one,	COR 5.6.153
And for thy sake have I shed many a tear,	1H6 5.4.19
And thus I prophesy, that many a thousand	3H6 5.6.37
And many an old man's sigh and many a widow's	3H6 5.6.39
There's many a gentle person made a Jack.	R3 1.3.72
Herself, the land, and many a Christian soul,	R3 4.4.408

But **whenever** it appears as the **first foot of a line**, it is inverted and it gets **three syllables**, just as we normally say it: **MEH-nee-uh**.

    – u /u – /

Many a man would take you at your word.	COE 1.2.17
Many a time he danc'd thee on his knee,	TIT 5.3.161
Many a morning hath he there been seen,	ROM 1.1.131
Many a duteous and knee-crooking knave	OTH 1.1.45
Many a bounteous year, must be employ'd	TIM 3.3.20
Many a battle have I won in France	3H6 1.2.73
Many a widow's husband groveling lies,	KJ 2.1.305
Many a poor man's son would have lien still,	KJ 4.1.50
Many a time hath banish'd Norfolk fought	R2 4.1.92
Many a nobleman lies stark and stiff	1H4 5.3.40
Many a groaning throe. Thus hulling in	H8 2.4.199
Many a dry drop seem'd a weeping tear,	LUC.1375

When "many a" appears at the start of a line, it is <u>always</u> an inverted foot. It is <u>never</u> part of an inversion when it falls in any other position.

I suspect the pronunciation changes when the phrase goes into inversion position in order to enhance the **swoop**. Those three syllables make a great attack phrase. The two-syllable version is much softer.

INVISIBLE CONTRACTIONS

There are hundreds of necessary contractions in Shakespeare that didn't make it into print. Be suspicious, when you see "I am" or "I have" or "I would" or any such phrase. It might need to be contracted. Let the scansion tell you for sure. If you read just as printed, you'll have hundreds of lumpy extra syllables.

Here are a few examples. Drill these until you are very sensitive to them.

And now be it known to you my full intent. (be't)	TIT 4.2.150
I have it! It is engendered! Hell and night (have't)	OTH 1.3.397
I thought as much; he would be above the clouds. (he'd)	2H6 2.1.15
I may be heard, I would crave a word or two, (I'd)	COR 3.1.281
That men shall swear I have discontinued school (I've)	MV 3.4.75
I have gone all night. Faith, I'll lie down and sleep. (I've)	CYM 4.2.294
I have seen the dumb men throng to see him, and (I've)	COR 2.1.254
Thus would I eat it.	TIM 4.3.284
Here, I will mend thy feast. (I'll)	TIM 4.3.284
My Lord, I am more amazed at his dishonor (I'm)	MM 5.1.377
I am wondrous merry-hearted, I could laugh now. (I'm)	TNK 2.1.105
But that I am bound in charity against it! (I'm)	H8 3.2.298
O Romeo, Romeo, brave Mercutio is dead! (Mercutio's)	ROM 3.1.116
She had all the royal makings of a queen, (She'd)	H8 4.1.87
And did forsake her. She had a song of willow; (She'd)	OTH 4.3.27

Name Cleopatra as she is called in Rome. (she's)	ANT 1.2.107
She is wondrous fair.	TNK 2.1.202
She is all the beauty extant. (She's, twice)	TNK 2.1.202
They are harsh and heavy to me.	H8 4.2.95.1
Do you note (They're)	H8 4.2.95.2
Thou art pinch'd for't now, Sebastian. Flesh and blood, (Th'art)	TEM 5.1.74
They are here in readiness.	CYM 4.2.336
But what from Rome? (They're)	CYM 4.2.336
Gloucester, thou wilt answer this before the Pope (thou'lt)	1H6 1.3.52
(Gloucester = GLOSS-tuhr; 1ST ft. inv.)	
Spirits of peace, where are ye? Are ye all gone? (y'all)	H8 4.2.83
Ye appear in everything may bring my ruin! (y'appear)	H8 3.2.242
You are sent for to the capitol. 'Tis thought (You're)	COR 2.1.252
You have holp to ravish your own daughters and (You've)	COR 4.6.82
You have done a brave deed. Ere you go, hear this: (You've)	COR 4.2.38

There are hundreds of these in the thirty-eight plays. When you find a line that doesn't want to scan, this is one of the first places to look. You see that there is a certain pattern here, certain kinds of phrase that Shakespeare contracts so often that he took it for granted and trusted his actors to take care of it. If you don't notice, if you speak these lines as printed, your sound will be like lumpy gravy. Scan carefully.

"AMER-ADDS": WORDS TO WHICH AMERICANS TEND TO ADD AN UNWANTED SYLLABLE

Here are a few examples of what I call **"Amer-Adds"**: words Shakespeare wants pronounced as one syllable but to which Americans often add a syllable. (Example: "FY-yuhr" for "fire" or "TAY-uhl" for "tale" or "FEE-uhl" for "feel." Each should normally be one syllable.) Those who have the two-syllable habit are usually locked into the pattern. They have trouble even noticing the difference. Only drill will solve this problem: weed out the old habit and root a new one. Speak aloud and listen carefully to yourself; be sure you're only giving the words one syllable.

wheel	feel	stale	stool	mild	wild
rail	reel	seal	fire	dire	sire
mire	hire	ire	our	hour	sour
vile	file	mile	vial	vail	vale
fail	frail	brier	coil	foil	spoil
foul	fool	scale	quail	whale	smile
yield	gale	child	meal	choir	owl
noise	world	steel	steal	soil	toil

Well, I told you it would be hard. But don't cut yourself any slack. Learn to do it with one syllable. Here are a few verse lines for practice. Each has at least one Amer-Add.

That spirit upon whose weal depends and rests	(spirit & weal)	HAM 3.3.14
Death on the wheel, or at wild horses' heels,	(wheel & wild)	COR 3.2.2
One fire drives out one fire; one nail one nail.	(fire & nail)	COR 4.7.54
Safest in shame; if fool'd, by fool'ry thrive.	(fool'd & fool'ry)	AW 4.3.328
That this same child of honor and renown,	(child)	1H4 3.2.139
The triple pillar of the world transformed	(world)	ANT 1.1.12
We make a quire, as doth the prison'd bird	(quire=choir)	CYM 3.3.43

To kindle cowards and to steel with valour	(steel)	JC 2.1.121
Unless thou yield thee as my prisoner.	(yield)	1H4 5.3.10
Here's such a coil. Come, what says Romeo?	(coil) (LW-VAR)	ROM 2.5.65
Each envious brier his weary legs do scratch.	(brier=briar)	VEN 705
No noise, but silence and eternal sleep.	(noise)	TIT 1.1.158
'Twere a perpetual spoil; and till we called	(spoil)	COR 2.2.118
Unapt to toil or trouble in the world	(toil & world)	SHR 5.2.165
By playing it to me with so sour a face.	(sour & playing)	ROM 2.5.24
Madam, an hour before the worshiped sun	(hour)	ROM 1.1.118
This love feel I that feel no love in this.	(feel)	ROM 1.1.182
Welcome, my lord; I marvel our mild husband	(our & mild)	KL 4.2.1

SCANSION TWO

We've covered the basics. You should be ready to face the most complex of Shakespeare's scripts as a true collaborator. But several subtler skills remain to be added to your repertoire and several traps lurk in your path, ready to subvert your journey. This sections aims to fill your quiver and inoculate you.

HOW DO YOU STAY CLEAR AND NATURAL WHILE MAINTAINING VERSE INTEGRITY?

> **If the audience can't feel the beginning and end of the verse line, then there is no verse line.**
>
> **If there is no verse line, you're speaking prose.**
>
> **You must cue the audience: this is the beginning; this is the end.**
>
> **Subliminally, but clearly.**

The beginning cue is hardest to talk about. We call it "**attack**." There is a special energy that belongs to the beginning of a line, a special surge of meaning which is subtle but recognizable, particularly when the previous line has ended appropriately.

You can't treat the start of a line just as you do every other foot. It's the start of something new and we have to hear that.

The surest thing we know about the line end is that there must be a **pause**.

A very small pause will do, but there must be a pause of some length and we must feel it.

The surest thing we know about the pause is that it must be justified by the actor's subtext. It can't be a merely mechanical pause. That would be deadly. There are many ways to pause and many reasons to pause. It's your creative work to find the perfect pause.

When there is a "**stop**" at the end of a line, it's easy and natural to pause. (A **stop** is the end of a major meaning unit, a place where you would expect to find a period or a ; or ? or !.)

We get into trouble when the verse line ends without a stop, when the thought seems to flow on into the next verse line, when the line ends in a comma or with no punctuation. At these points, the actor's creativity is put to the test. Our old habits of prose speech take over and the verse disappears. We "**run on**," as it's called. When we run on at the end of the line, the audience has no way to keep its verse bearings. It hears prose. The solution in this situation is the technique I call **THE LILT** (see p. 47)

TESTIMONY OF ONE OF THE GREAT DIRECTORS

Shakespeare's architecture in his verse is entirely dependent on the preservation of the iambic line. His form is destroyed by acting single words rather than lines. This may come from a wholly laudable desire to make the audience understand an archaic word. But it chops up the line and loses the energy . . . . Chopping up lines into little naturalistic gobbets may sound 'modern' but it plays hell with the meaning. And by chopping it up, the actors begin to communicate in irregular phrases rather than in the full iambic line. Consequently the actor becomes slower than the audience. The sanctity of the line is betrayed and Shakespeare's primary means of giving out information rapidly and holding our attention is destroyed.

Peter Hall in his *Shakespeare's Advice to the Players*

THE ROOT OF GOOD ACTING

The fundamental requirements of good acting are few and simple:

KNOW WHAT YOU MEAN.
MEAN WHAT YOU SAY.

Know **precisely** what you mean, in every second, by every word, by every move.

Mean what you say in the most **active** possible sense: speak and move in order to **control** the world (the world out there or the one inside) in some very **specific** way. Speak with the character's purposes, with his or her attitudes, not with yours.

This applies to all acting. It's easier to say than to do. It seems to be even harder with Shakespeare because we are in awe of him and this short-circuits our understandings. And our concern to get the technical matters right distracts us.

For reasons I don't quite understand, many actors are willing to violate these rules when they play Shakespeare. They will say lines without knowing exactly what they mean and they will say them for no purpose but to fulfill their obligation to say them.

Shakespeare is the greatest but he can't survive this. No playwright can do it alone. If you want to bring his heroic plays to life, you must act as organically as you ever have. You must know more than general meanings and moods.

You must **know precisely what each word must accomplish and why your character needs just that word.**

DON'T SELL YOUR TALENT SHORT.

IF YOU DON'T KNOW, ASK.

Here's the rule:

> **Never perform a line without knowing**
> - precisely what it means,
> - to whom you are saying it,
> - why you are saying it, in the deepest sense, and
> - how you feel about the topic,
>   your listener, and yourself.

ENEMIES OF SHAPE AND COLOR

The most common feedback after workshop performances, whether it comes from me, from the performers, or from the audience is **"it needs more Shape and Color."** Every performer seems to feel this as he or she performs. It is deeply frustrating to everyone. We know that there is potential for excitement in everything we perform and we can hear that it isn't coming through fully. This flatness comes from these things:

INHIBITION: We are all uncertain of our ability to rise up to the demands of Shakespeare. **Fear** gets a pretty good grip on us. We're **distracted**. We do what all people do when facing a challenge we're not sure we can meet: we tighten up to avoid mistakes. But acting absolutely requires relaxation, spontaneity, and focus, all of which are squelched by fear and the inhibition which springs from it.

UNREADINESS: Our fear makes our preparation harder. We worry about learning the words and remembering the rhythm. The worry almost guarantees that we will have memory problems. When we have memory problems, we lose our subtext and it is the subtext which generates most of the meaning. And so we flatten. It is necessary to "hyper-prepare" for Shakespearean performance. We need to be so solid and confident and committed to our characters' purposes that nothing can take us away from the moment.

INADEQUATE SUBTEXT: At first, we all have trouble understanding Shakespeare's words. Too often we settle for a "general idea" of the meaning of the words and so our subtext is inevitably impoverished. **Simplification and over-generalization are the death of acting.** We can't be eloquent when we don't know precisely what we're saying. We won't really play our roles until we understand every nuance of meaning in every phrase. That's not easy but there are plenty of places to get help.

MODERN SPEECH QUIRKS

This is where the big problems begin.

The language and the meanings and the verse should be the basic shapers of our speech. Also, the style of the time and place of the play and the character should influence us.

Unfortunately, there is another very strong force which intrudes and shapes our speech inappropriately: every culture, sub-culture, and individual has habits of speech which overlay, and sometimes contradict, the influence of meaning and verse. These habits are merely quirks; arbitrary, unnecessary and often contradictory to clear meaning.

Most of us are so rooted in these modern habits that we are unaware of them. The impulses that spring from these habits often seem like the demands of meaning but they're not. This can put us in conflict with Shakespeare's meanings and verse. This is why some people just can't act period plays: they are so locked into modern quirks that they can't let go.

Here are two Modern Speech Quirks that trip us up so often that I call them "traps." They are:

THE "NOT-TRAP"

> For some reason, we love to kick the heck out of every "not" we see. Shakespeare, on the other hand, hardly ever emphasizes "not." Don't fall into the trap of making "not" an inherently emphatic word. Let "not" be relatively emphatic only when your scanning says it must be.

The "Not-Trap"

Shakespeare felt it was almost always better to put the relatively strong emphasis on the verb that was modified by the "not." Try these lines, none of which have emphatic "not"s, and see what happens. All are stock blank verse except for one feminine ending ("better").

Day serves not night more faithful than I'll be.	PER 1.2.110
We do not look for rev'rence but for love.	PER 1.4.99
Now, by the gods, he could not please me better.	PER 2.3.72
I will not have excuse with saying this.	PER 2.3.96
And if I fail not in my deep intent,	R3 1.1.149
And this fell tempest shall not cease to rage. ("shall" outweighs "not")	2H6 3.1.351
A subtle knave, but yet it shall not serve. (ditto)	2H6 2.1.103

Drill these lines until they feel like the normal, best way to express the thought. Then intersperse them with a few of the rare emphatic-not lines. Set for yourself the habit of finding rhythm in the meter and the meaning rather than in old habits.

"Not" is emphatic when the meaning needs it to be emphatic. It is not an inherently emphatic word. Shakespeare will tell you when it is useful to make it relatively emphatic.

Here are a few lines with relatively strong "not"s. It is fun to start with some "shall <u>not</u>"s which reverse the usual emphasis pattern:

The world shall not be ransom for thy life. ("not" outweighs "shall")	2H6 3.2.297
The sly slow hours shall not determinate. (ditto)	R2 1.3.150
And not a thought but thinks on dignity.	2H6 3.1.338
Will not conclude their plotted tragedy.	2H6 3.1.153

Make "not" a relatively emphatic syllable only when Shakespeare puts it in that position . . . which he doesn't often do. Scan carefully. Don't let Modern Quirks rule your speech.

THE "PERSONAL PRONOUN-TRAP"

> We also over-kick the pronouns. We just love "I" and "me" and "you" and "she" and on and on. We can't seem to resist the temptation to push them hard. Shakespeare's meanings, however, very seldom allow this. Scan your lines and kick the pronouns only when asked to by the verse.

Emphatic personal pronouns are rare in Shakespeare's scripts.
Speak these lines without analyzing them in advance.

I give my cause who best can justify . . .	PER Chorus.1.42
One sin, I know, another doth provoke.	PER 1.1.138
How dearly would it touch thee to the quick . . .	COE 2.2.139
Not all these lords do vex me half so much . . .	2H6 1.3.73

Did you find yourself inclined to emphasize either of the "I"s or "thee" or "me"? Most actors would. None of these are emphatic pronouns. All of these are standard blank verse lines and all of the pronouns fall in the relatively unemphatic position.

Here is a line which actors find very surprising at first but it is Shakespeare's way and it makes wonderful sense: the emphatic "from" with two relatively unemphatic personal pronouns surrounding. Think of "possess from" as a kind of compound verb.

If aught possess thee from me it is dross.	COE 2.2.186

Almost every actor wants to say "thee from me," which not only ruins the rhythm but misses the meaning. ("Possess thee from" means, roughly, "takes you away.")

Actors struggle with this next one. They feel they must punch "thou." But Shakespeare never allows a ninth syllable more emphatic than the tenth.

> How can I then be elder than thou art?   SONN 22.8

Drill these lines until the relatively unemphatic personal pronoun feels normal. Then intersperse lines, which do have relatively emphatic pronouns with the more typical lines until you become habituated with the practice of discovering the emphasis in the meter and the meaning. Here are a few lines with relatively emphatic pronouns:

> But thy eternal summer shall not fade, (Still a light "not.")   SONN 18.9
> Which in thy breast doth live, as thine in me, (1 lighter, 2 & 3 heavier)   SONN 22.7
> But I, that am not shaped for sportive tricks.   R3 1.1.14
> And leave the world for me to bustle in.   R3 1.1.152

These last two are Richard III. One clever way Shakespeare characterizes him is by giving him an amazing number of relatively emphatic personal pronouns. If actors routinely emphasize pronouns, they not only violate the verse rhythm but also rob Shakespeare of this valuable tool.

These are just two of the damaging Modern Speech Quirks. There are plenty more. You will be tempted to think that these habits are necessary for meaning. They aren't. Your Shakespeare will be clear only if you follow **his** speech habits.

It's not enough to know about the danger of Modern Speech Quirks. It takes disciplined drill to break these habits. The first step is to notice it when you fall into one of these traps, or into any violation of the verse rhythm. Then ask yourself whether Modern Speech Habits may be the cause.

Shakespeare's Verse: A User's Manual

> **If your intuition tells you that a line should be said differently than the verse requires, if it feels "odd" or "unnatural" to say the line Shakespeare's way, either you are the victim of an irrelevant modern habit or you have misunderstood the line.**

The moral of this story is **trust Shakespeare**. Understand him and follow his lead; he'll give you everything you need to be fascinating and eloquent.

THERE ARE NO QUICK SYLLABLES IN BLANK VERSE: THE DIDDLEY MENACE

The tossing away of some syllables by shortening them extremely is a modern habit which doesn't work for Shakespeare's verse. We have light syllables and heavy syllables and syllables in between. We have coarse syllables and refined syllables. We have super-long syllables and many other kinds of syllables. We have fast tempos. But we have no quick, short, thrown-away, tossed-off syllables. No grace-note syllables. Every syllable, light or heavy, coarse or fine, loud or soft, gets its full length. Or the rhythm dies.

This is true when Shakespeare is writing iambic pentameter or trochaic tetrameter, as he sometimes does, or any of the other syllabic verse forms he experimented with in the early days.

Shakespeare also experimented, rarely, with **Accentual Verse**, in which only the major accents of the line are counted and quick syllables are acceptable. Let's take another look at the example of this form drawn from *Comedy of Errors* on pages 49 and 50.

DIDDLEYS

That's what I call the short rhythm bursts that result from clustering two or three short syllables together. A DIDDLEY is really a rushed dactyl, a kind of verse foot Shakespeare doesn't use.

When a Diddley appears in a Blank Verse line it disrupts it. **– uu**, Diddley. Listen carefully for them. They are a common part of modern prose speech but they have no place here.

You'll be most tempted to Diddley when you come to phrases with two or three short words in a row, such as the "Will you" of "Will you go sister."

In common speech, we are used to squeezing phrases such as "Do you want to" into "D'yawana," almost swallowing the words.

Here's a likely Diddle-line:
>   To creep in at mine eyes. Well, let it be.   (in at)   TN 1.5.287

The first danger is "in at mine," a major Diddle-trap. And "let it be" is an attractive trap. Try squeezing those phrases and then try to scan them without inflating them to normal size.

Here is a line that tempts terribly: In *Twelfth Night*, Viola says
>   I am the man. If it be so, as 'tis,   TN 2.2.25

"I am the man" tempts us to rush and "if it be so" mercilessly seduces those with a prose inclination. But those with a sense of verse and a grasp of the wonderful mind of Viola will find a much richer music in the fully drawn out and inhabited syllables of these short words.

It's not only short words which suffer the wrath of the Diddley. There are many words we are just used to hurrying and we stay with the habit when we speak verse. Later in the same speech, Viola says:

> Wherein the pregnant enemy does much.   TN 2.2.28

"Enemy" is a word we normally squnch into three quick, short syllables: into a Diddley. If we say it this way, the balance of the line is thrown off. "Enemy" deserves its full music.

Sonnet 76 is loaded with Diddle-traps. I count five lines which provide major opportunities to ruin the rhythmic scheme. For example:

> Why with the time do I not glance aside?   SONN 76.3

"Why with the" is an inviting inverted Diddley trap. "Do I not" tempts us to Diddley "do I" into "d'wi" and inappropriately punch "not."

> To new found methods and to compounds strange.   SONN 76.4

"And to" is an almost irresistible temptation but properly drawn out, it sings.

Close behind in the Book of Diddley Golden Oldies comes "in a," also found in Sonnet 76.

> And keep invention in a noted weed   SONN 76.6

It would be a good idea to copy and keep Sonnet 76 handy as a practice piece until you acquire a strong habit of fully valuing all your words.

And finally, a great climactic line from *Henry 5* which the Diddley would deflate. Don't invert "more than" but keep the line building and don't Diddle "more than did" or "laugh at it" because those Diddleys have a miniaturizing effect.

> When thousands weep more than did laugh at it.   H5 2.2.297

DIDDLEY WORK

> Here are examples of lines with word clusters
> which will tempt you to Diddley.
>
> Beware. Practice giving full value to each syllable in each verse line.
> There are no short syllables in Shakespeare's verse.

This first group features lines with "in a," one of the most diddlicious clusters, then a group with "do I."

That in a spleen unfolds both heaven and earth,	MND	1.1.146
And sometime lurk I in a gossip's bowl		2.1.47
Forsook his scene and entered in a brake,		3.2.15
And even for that do I love you the more.		2.1.202
To conjure tears up in a poor maid's eyes		3.2.158
When in a wood of Crete they bayed the bear		4.1.112
Sees Helen's beauty in a brow of Egypt.		5.1.11
He wears his honour in a box unseen	AWW	2.3.277
Is wicked meaning in a lawful deed,		3.7.45
And lawful meaning in a lawful act,		3.7.46
Wrapped in a paper which contained the name		5.3.94
I'll set thee in a shower of gold, and hail	ANT	2.5.45
A certain queen to Caesar in a mattress.		2.6.70
Hereafter, in a better world than this,	AYL	1.2.273
Never so much as in a thought unborn		1.3.49
To say he'll turn your current in a ditch	COR	3.1.96

O, speak of that! That do I long to hear.	HAM	2.2.50
Or rather do I not in plainest truth		2.1.200
O my dear mother, do I see you living?		5.3.317
But wherefore do I tell these news to thee?	4H1	3.2.121
Nor do I as an enemy to peace	4H2	4.2.61
And tidings do I bring, and lucky joys,		5.3.95
Nor other satisfaction do I crave	6H1	2.3.76
Stay, go, do what you will – the like do I		4.5.50
Thus do I hope to shake King Henry's head.	6H3	1.1.20
For in thy shoulder do I build my seat,		2.6.100
Why, am I dead? Do I not breathe a man?		3.1.8
So do I wish the crown, being so far off;		3.2.140
Over thy wounds now do I prophesy –	JC	3.1.259
In right of Arthur do I claim of thee.	KJ	2.1.153
Alas, poor fool, why do I pity him	TGV	4.4.90
And to say true, I stole it. Do I pinch you?	TNK	3.6.55
Or do I dream? Or have I dreamed till now?	SHR	intro 2.69
But in the other's silence do I see		1.1.70

A SPECIAL CASE OF DIDDLEYS: "...ABLE"

Shakespeare was fond of words ending in "able." Over eight hundred times he used words ending that way. He had three different ways of pronouncing them: fifty-four of the words used in verse sound familiar to us; they rhyme with "a **bull**," for example, "syllable." Sixty-three of the verse words seem a bit odd to most of us at first: they rhyme with "**bub**ble." Just a few words, usually short ones, rhyme with "table."

We have two problems with these bubble-words: we tend to Diddley them and we emphasize the bubble-words on the wrong syllable, like bull-words, shattering the rhythm of the line. Shakespeare's favorite bubble-word was "honorable," which he uses 131 times. Most of us are inclined to say ON-ur-uh-BULL, rushing the first three syllables. But all these lines ask us for ON-or-UH-bull. Try this line:

> You need but plead your honorable priv'lege.   AWW 4.5.88

Give each of the syllables its full value and let "UH" top "or" and "bull" to get full value from the line.

Shakespeare touches all our moods. Another of his favorite bubble-words is "miserable," also a powerful Diddle-trap. We are mightily tempted to slip-slide quickly through all four syllables, kicking only the first: MIZ-uhr-uh-bull. But Shakespeare asks for **MIZ**-uh-RUH-bull, with each syllable given full length, which not only captures the verse power but enhances the onomatopoetic impact, making us feel the idea.

Try this line. See how easy it is to Diddley it, then do it *without* short syllables and *with* the bubble.

> From MIZ-uhr-uh-bull slumber I awaked   AYL 4.3.133
> From **MIZ**-uh-RUH-bull slumber I awaked

A Special Case of Diddleys: "... Able"

Most of us have a very strong "a **bull**" habit. Only drill breaks habits. You may need to exaggerate a bit at first as you work to break your old habit and build a new one. You will soon become less self-conscious about speaking the bubble words correctly and as you do you will find that they are not odd or distracting but effective enhancers of your verse power.

Here are some useful lists to help you in your scansion labors. First, lists of the bubble words with sample verse lines for each. Drill them till you are a master.

"ABLE" WORDS RHYMING WITH "BUBBLE" (‾ ᵕ)

FOUR-SYLLABLE WORDS:

accep**ta**ble	**de**tes**ta**ble	marketable	serviceable
admi**ra**ble	**es**ti**ma**ble	med'cinable	sociable (yes, 4)
amiable	**ex**ecra**ble**	memorable	tolerable
answe**ra**ble	fashionable	miserable	variable
chari**ta**ble	favorable	penetrable	venerable
comfor**ta**ble	honorable	perdurable	veritable
commen**da**ble	hospitable	profitable	vulnerable
demon**stra**ble	lamentable	reasonable	

How **hon**orable and how kindly we	ANT 5.1.58
O gross and **mi**serable ignorance!	2H6 4.2.159
I come to thee for **char**itable licence,	H5 4.7.69
O comfortable Friar! Where is my lord?	ROM 5.3.148
My reasonable part produces reason	KJ 3.4.54
And, commendable proved, let's die in pride.	1H6 4.6.57
I know thee well: a serviceable villain,	KL 4.6.252
Whiles he is vaulting variable ramps,	CYM 1.7.134
As venerable Nestor, hatched in silver,	TC 1.3.65

With profitable labor to his grave:	H5 4.1.270
Death! Death, O amiable, lovely death!	KJ 3.4.25
And I will kiss thy detestable bones	KJ 3.4.29
Lend favorable ears to our request,	R3 3.7.100
But penetrable to your kind entreaties,	R3 3.7.224
Is a plain fish, and no doubt marketable.	TEM 5.1.266
But, howsoever, strange and admirable.	MND 5.1.27
O perdurable shame! Let's stab ourselves.	H5 4.5.7
And all things answerable to this portion.	TS 2.1.352
Tell thou the lamentable tale of me,	R2 5.1.44
Than the constraint of hospitable zeal	KJ 2.1.244
Some griefs are med'cinable, that is one of them,	CYM 3.2.33
He sends you this most memorable line,	H5 2.4.88
Your acceptable greeting to my king.	E3 1.2.39

FIVE-SYLLABLE WORDS:

Now drill these till five-syllable bubble-words feel normal.

a**bom**inable	inhabitable	irreparable	unquestionable
dis**com**fortable	inhospitable	irrevocable	unreasonable
dis**hon**orable	innumerable	proportionable	unseparable
im**pen**etrable	in**sep**erable	uncomfortable	unseasonable
incomparable	in**so**ciable	unmeritable	unserviceable
inevitable	in**tol**erable	unmitigable	unvenerable
in**ex**ecrable	in**vi**olable	unpardonable	unviolable
inexorable	invulnerable	unprofitable	

A Special Case of Diddleys: "...Able"

Despiteful and in**tole**r**a**ble wrongs!	TIT 4.4.50
To find ourselves dis**ho**no**ra**ble graves.	JC 1.2.137
Abominable Gloucester, guard thy head;	1H6 1.3.87
And, with thy hand, thy faith irrevocable	3H6 3.3.247
For it is as the air invulnerable,	HAM 1.1.146
Come, come, no more of this unprofitable chat. (6 ft.)	1H4 3.1.59
What man is there so much unreasonable,	MV 5.1.203
Must yield to such inevitable shame	MV 4.1.57
Unseparable, shall within this hour,	COR 4.4.16
O, 'tis a fault too too unpardonable!	3H6 1.4.106
More fierce and more inexorable far	ROM 5.3.38
As if they vowed some league inviolable;	3H6 2.1.30
A merchant of incomparable wealth.	SHR 4.2.98
Then, that you've sent innumerable substance	H8 3.2.326
This is a slight unmeritable man,	JC 4.1.12
Dark, deadly, silent, and uncomfortable.	E3 4.5.18

And one lonely six-syllable word: Undistinguishable

These things seem small and **un**dis**tin**gui**sha**ble,	MND 4.1.186

And here is a list of the words used in verse that welcome you to use "a-BULL."

"ABLE" WORDS RHYMING WITH "A BULL" (ŭ −)

Practice the emphasis patterns. I've bolded the first fifteen words to make your work easier. Once you get the feel of the "a-BULL" words, create a new collection which randomly mixes words from each of the categories. Practice them. Work for speed of recognition.

affa**ble**	liable	tractable
as**sail**a**ble**	mirable	tuneable
at**temp**ta**ble**	mockable	unagreeable
capa**ble**	movable	unassailable
changeable	mutable	uncapable
con**form**a**ble**	notable	uncurbable
consta**ble**	oathable	unmatchable
damna**ble**	palpable	unmeasurable
de**ceiv**a**ble**	passable	unprizeable
de**mon**stra**ble**	portable	unreconcilable
Dunsta**ble**	potable	unremoveable
ex**cus**a**ble**	probable	unscalable
im**pregn**a**ble**	razorable (3 sylls)	unshunnable
in**ca**pa**ble**	rebukeable	unspeakable
in**clin**a**ble**	remarkable	unsuitable
incurable	semblable	unswayable
inexplicable	sociable (3 this time)	untireable
irremovable	suitable	untuneable
inscrutable	syllable	unwedgeable
insupportable	tenable	
laudable	traceable	

Finally, here is a short list of words which rhyme with "table."

able	fable	stable
abler	table	unable
cable	tabled	unstable
disable	sable	

FLOWING AND CHOPPING

Shakespeare's verse needs to FLOW. You will find tremendous variety in it but always it flows. If you understand the difference between **legato** and **staccato** in music, understand that Shakespeare's verse is much like legato music: there is continuity from note to note, from word to word. It may crash and bang or it may whisper but **it always flows.**

We destroy the continuity of the verse when we CHOP. To Chop is to make abrupt stops at places other than periods or other full stops. We can achieve all of the slowing down and speeding up we need without Chopping. What we do is create a **flowing** verse line which **evolves** from moment to moment instead of leaping. It evolves from one tempo to another, one texture to another, one tone to another, but always it flows. It is not atomized. We vocally sustain the words and other sounds.

This does not mean that all the verse is "prettified" and lyrical. This sustained flow covers the full range of moods and textures.

UNWANTED PAUSES

One of the tricks of modern naturalistic acting is to pause or breathe in the middle of phrases, putting brief silences in places other than Caesuras where they do not match the sense of the line (though they may convey the subtext of the line). Contemporary writers have a standard device to show their desire for this trick: the "three-dot" signal. ("Shucks Maggie. I just . . . love ya so much I want to . . . aw, heck.") But Shakespeare doesn't use or allow this trick. When we act verse, we should give it up. We don't need it and it destroys the rhythmic flow of the verse, shattering the beat. Shakespeare knows when pauses are most effective and he tells us clearly.

MOMENTUM WORDS AT THE START OF LINES

Here's another Shakespearean form which Modern Habit often makes us mis-speak. He begins many sentences with **a short word** ("well" or "come" or "nay" or "now" or "ay" or "hark" or "why" and so on) which in your text is usually **followed by a comma**. Like this:

    Alack, 'tis he! Why, he was met e'en now   KL 4.4.1

Modern habit makes us want to say "Alack . . . 'tis he" or "Well . . . I will go" or "Nay . . . fear not me" with a very emphatic "Alack" or "Well" or "Nay."

> **Shakespeare wants us to do just the opposite: a light first word, rushing quickly into a more emphatic second. Think of the first word as a sort of warm-up, to give us momentum for a high energy move into the line. Never take a "thought-pause" or suspension in such a situation.**

The same is true when he gives us word repetitions such as "Come, come" or "Ay, ay" or "Now, now." Don't say "Come . . . (*pause to see if he's coming or not*) come." Make it a standard iambic foot and speak it quickly. The repetition is there to accelerate the momentum, not to give us two shots at the thought.

Glide into the second syllable and emphasize the second more than the first, making a proper iamb.

But wait a minute, you say. If Shakespeare didn't want some kind of pause, why did he put the commas there? Good question. The answer is even better: he didn't. Most of us who study these things believe that Shakespeare punctuated for the actor, not the grammar teacher. Much can be learned by studying the original punctuation and spelling, even though we know that some of what we inherited must be blamed on the typesetters, not on William. The commas and many other punctuation "improvements" are the gifts of editors with a greater interest in formal grammar than in the nuances of expression. These intrusions appear as early as in the Rowe edition of the works in 1709.

However, the original printings give us so many lines beginning with these small, attention-getting words **not** followed by a comma that we can say with confidence that Shakespeare intended neither the comma nor the pause. Here are a few lines given both as they typically appear in modern editions (1st) and as they were first published (2nd).

What, have you writ that letter to my sister? What have you writ that letter to my sister?	KL 1.4.331
Now, fair Hippolyta, our nuptial hour Now faire Hippolita, our nuptial hower	MND 1.1.1
Nay, get thee in. I'll pray and then I'll sleep. Nay get thee in; Ile pray and then Ile sleepe.	KL 3.4.27
Nay, press not so upon me, stand far off. Nay presse not so upon me, stand farre off.	JC 3.2.168
Ay, my good lord, 'twas he informed against him, I my good lord: 'twas he inform'd against him,	KL 4.2.92
Hark, Polydore, it sounds. But what occasion (Hearke Polidore) it sounds: but what occasion	CYM 4.2.187

And on and on. You get the point? Shakespeare sent us no indication that he wanted a pause. Once you get the habit of the comma-free momentum words, you will feel the rightness of this approach. You'll learn to love the way they lift and speed your performance.

Momentum Words at the Start of Lines

Here are some practice lines to help you break the habit. Drill these.

Yea, or so many, sith both charge and danger	KL 2.4.234
Why, after I have cut the egg i'th'middle	KL 1.4.156
Come, wait upon him. Lead him to my bower	MND 3.1.192
What, fifty of my foll'wers at a clap?	KL 1.4.291
Well, you may fear too far.	KL 1.4.325
Safer than trust too far.	KL 1.4.325
What, did my father's godson seek your life?	KL 2.1.90
Come, let's in all.	KL 3.4.175
This way my Lord.	KL 3.4.175
With Him.	KL.3.4.175
No, my good lord; I met him back again	KL 4.2.90
Yea, every idle, nice, and wanton reason,	2H4 4.1.189
What, canst thou not forbear me half an hour?	2H4 4.5.110
No, Cassius: For the eye sees not itself	JC 1.2.52
What, have I pinched you Signor Gremio?	SHR 2.1.364
Nay, get thee gone. Two things are to be done.	OTH 2.3.371
Nay get thee in. I'll pray and then I'll sleep.	KL 3.4.27
Ay, my good lord – "my lord" I should say rather.	3H6 5.6.2
Yea, this man's brow, like to a title-leaf,	2H4 1.1.60

Did you manage to ignore the commas? Did you resist the temptation?
Good; you're on your way to a bright, high-energy reading.

TESTIMONY OF THE BRILLIANT AND FAMOUS

"... when the actors start stretching the lines and taking naturalistic pauses, you want to scream 'Get on with it, for God's sake,' because the pulse of the iambic pentameter is like a heartbeat. See Judi Dench doing Shakespeare. Musically she moves the beat about, but she doesn't add extra bars of thinking time. That's what's so exhilarating ... in stage productions of Shakespeare, dialogue controls all the muscles ... the verse is the pulse of his plays .... neglect it at your peril."

Richard Eyre, former Head, Royal National Theatre, England

BREATHING AND PAUSING

The best Shakespearean actors take pauses only when the grammatical form of the line allows it, at the period preferably, at the semi-colon if needed. Any other breath shatters the integrity of the line, disrupts flow.

THE LONG-LINE CHALLENGE

The trained actor of Shakespeare breathes only at periods. He or she should be able to speak a sentence of seven verse lines without breathing. These lines are not long because Shakespeare got to rambling; he had a structure in mind for these complex thoughts that a breath pause would interrupt.

Most of us find the long-lines difficult at first but, with practice, any of us can learn to do it. Work on taking a <u>full</u> breath before beginning. Use all of the breath you have and don't slow down or pause unnecessarily. **When practicing, stop when you run out of breath. Don't sneak little breaths.** Speak out fully; don't fool yourself by speaking at movie-actor volume. Use the following lines for practice. Perform the bold-type sections.

Macbeth from *Macbeth*, 3.1:

> So is he mine, and in such bloody distance,
> That every minute of his being thrusts
> Against my near'st of life; **and though I could**
> **With barefac'd power sweep him from my sight,**
> **And bid my will avouch it, yet I must not,**
> **For certain friends that are both his and mine,**
> **Whose loves I may not drop, but wail his fall**
> **Who I myself struck down.**

OK, so you probably couldn't do it on one breath the first time you tried. You might not be able to do it the tenth time. But it's like building muscle or losing fat. If you train yourself to do it, you will rise to a wonderful new level of vocal expressiveness. You'll find it easy to speak all of your lines without inappropriate breath pauses. The rhythms you have learned to discover will have deeper roots. Shakespeare's subtle rhythmic structures are powerful but fragile. Something as simple as a misplaced breath pause can turn the eloquent to the clumsy.

We don't misplace our breath pauses on purpose. We do it either because we're out of shape or because we haven't decided to collaborate with Shakespeare by breathing where he asks us to, or because we just don't notice when we are breathing.

- ☑ Work on these long lines.
- ☑ Learn to take a full breath each time. Most of us take in half our capacity.
- ☑ Learn to use all the breath you have. It takes muscle control beyond the usual.

Hamlet from his "Oh what a rogue" soliloquy (2.2):

> Is it not monstrous that this player here,
> But in a fiction, in a dream of passion,
> Could force his soul so to his own conceit
> That from her working all the visage wann'd
> Tears in his eyes, distraction in's aspect,
> A broken voice, and his whole function suiting
> With forms to his conceit? And all for nothing.

Oberon from *A Midsummer Night's Dream*, 2.1:

> Thou remb'rest
> Since once I sat upon a promont'ry
> And heard a mermaid on a dolphin's back
> Utt'ring such dulcet and harmonious breath
> That the rude sea grew civil at her song,

> And certain stars shot madly from their spheres
> To hear the sea-maid's music?

Othello to Iago (3.4):

> Like to the Pontic sea
> Whose icy current and compulsive course
> Ne'er feels retiring ebb, but keeps due on
> To the Propontic and the Hellespont,
> E'en so my bloody thoughts, with violent pace,
> Shall ne'er look back, ne'er ebb to humble love,
> Till that a capable and wide revenge
> Swallow them up.

VOWEL SHIFTS

Have you ever noticed that we all use little changes in pronunciation as a tool to get the rhythm of our feeling into our speech? We don't always pronounce the words the way the dictionary says we do, even those who are well trained in speech. We stretch or shrink words to make them feel right, to get the emphasis our purposes require.

One of the things we do is change the vowel sounds. For many words, we have a vowel we use when we want a syllable to be emphatic and a slightly different one for when we want it less emphatic. Some vowel sounds are inherently emphatic; these are the basic vowels we are taught as straight A, E, I, O, U. We have softer versions of each of these. Though most of us never consciously notice it, we shift back and forth according to our needs.

Unfortunately, most of us forget this subtle technique when we start speaking Shakespeare's verse. We are so determined to "speak properly" that we tend to use the straight vowel sounds all the time and this really gets in the way of Shakespeare's verse.

He counts on actors to do what we normally do: use the straight vowel sounds for more emphatic syllables and the softer versions for the less emphatic. For example, Shakespeare always uses the words "report" and "renew" with the heavier emphasis on the second syllable. If we pronounce the "**re**" of these words as "**ree**," we mask the iambic rhythm. Pronounce these words "ruh-**PORT**" and "ruh-**NYEW**." This sounds perfectly normal to the audience, clarifies the rhythm, and helps to convey the polish of the character. You can ignore this rule purposely as a way of suggesting a coarse, uneducated character. There are thousands of words to which this applies. Here are a few:

- ☑ Words like de**fense**, de**fect**, and de**feat** (de = **deh** or **duh**)
- ☑ Words starting with **a** or **ab** or **an** (not ab-**HOR** but uhb-**HOR**)
- ☑ Starting with **O** (not oh-**PHEEL**-ia or oh-**THEL**-oh but uh-**PHEEL**-ia and uh-**THEL**-oh or aw-**THEL**-oh)

And note two common words almost always mispronounced: "**ye**" and "**methinks**"; should be "**yuh**" and "**muh**-THINKS" unless in relatively emphatic position, which happens maybe 1% of uses. Those straight "e"s really cut through and force unwanted emphasis on us.

(Think about it; most of us say "yuh" for "you" much of the time. "Yuh like Shakespeare? Muhthinks he is the best!)

"O" AND "OH"

You will find many "O"s and "Oh"s in Shakespeare. It takes plenty of courage to play them the way Shakespeare intends. Don't think of these as "words" to be spoken as you would any other word. Shakespeare gives them to us as simple vowels sounds to serve as **the vehicle for our full vocal expression of large feelings**. When he gives you an "O" or "Oh," he wants you to **sing your feeling.**

When you find one of these words, first **take it as a clear clue that your character feels strongly and wants to share the feeling or can't stop it from escaping**. Decide what that feeling is and how powerful it is and then stretch, bend, twist the "O" sound to fit the feeling.

It takes plenty of nerve to do this because it is so unlike most of what we do on stage. However, it is something we do all the time in real life, not only with "O" but with many words. Overcome your resistance to the boldness of it. If you say "O" or "Oh" like an unimportant little word, it sounds old-fashioned and silly. If you **use** the sound, it becomes one of the high (heroic, energetic) moments of the play. This is the kind of challenge that separates the real actor from the would-be.

Oddly, no matter how much you make of these big "O"s, they are always the relatively unemphatic syllable in the foot. To make this work, we **segue** from the "O" to the following syllable with no space between. The "O" serves as a huge "wind-up" for our move into this more important word.

O, 'tis the spite of hell, the fiends arch-mock	OTH 4.1.70
O, that the slave had forty thousand lives!	OTH 3.3.439
O happy horse, to bear the weight of Ant'ny!	ANT 1.5.21
O indistinguish'd space of woman's will!	KL 4.6.270
O Caesar, what a wounding shame is this,	ANT 5.2.159
I know not where to turn. O welcome home!	COR 2.1.174

STRAIGHT "U" SOUNDS

A sad thing happening to American English is the gradual disappearance of our straight U sounds. We turn many of them to OO sounds and some to UH. It's an unfortunate loss. The straight U sound, also called "the liquid U," is the one you use when you say "music" or "cute" or "Cupid."

These are some words from *Romeo and Juliet* for which you may have lost the U sound. If you need to speak one of these words, practice saying it correctly. It's one of our most elegant sounds:

suit, lure, new, consume, tutor, fortune

If your role is lower-class, forget this.

Practice saying these words with the liquid U until they feel normal and easy.

Duke	duty	due	lute
allure	sure	venture	endure
censure	sue	assure	renew
pursue (2ND u only)			

If you're not used to the liquid U, it will feel odd to you. After a little practice, you'll feel comfortable and you'll come to like the pure sound. The sound is appropriate for educated and polished characters.

DIALECT

Speaking of odd pronunciation, American actors should beware the temptation to slip into British dialect. The British dialects you have heard have nothing to do with the way English was pronounced in Shakespeare's time. It's an affectation that feels artificial. Use whatever version of Standard American is appropriate for your character, region, personality, rank. Don't drop "r"s or round "o"s. (Standard American: a dialect that people don't recognize as coming from any particular region.) Of course, it is legitimate to set a play in a specific place, say, New Orleans, and choose all dialects from that pool.

WORDS, FIGURES OF SPEECH, RHETORIC

Great Shakespearean actors are wont to say "it is all in the words; everything you need, there in the words." And this is true, when you make your contact with them thorough, intimate and sensuous enough.

For example, there is a book full of crucial information for each of the plays coded in Shakespeare's choice of vowels and consonants. If you look carefully enough at these shifting choices, you'll be amazed how the playwright's vision opens up for you. You don't need a code book to read these meanings. Just pay deep attention to the sensual qualities of words you've previously taken for granted.

At the heart of education in Shakespeare's time was Rhetoric, the study of the power of language, written and spoken, to reach and move us. They codified the forms of language and drilled and drilled young students in each form until they mastered these tools. Even today the typical educated Brit makes most Americans look semi-literate and tongue-tied. It is their heritage. Some day, take a look at the list of hundreds of formal figures of speech with Latin names that Elizabethan students were expected not only to remember but also to use skillfully.

Shakespeare made the most of this education. He shows both mastery and delight in his use of the great figures. **We need to recognize and understand them if we are to use them effectively.** And herein lies a problem. People in our time are very impatient with the study of the mechanics of language. We're all for spontaneity and I would guess that most of us couldn't name or recognize three figures of speech let alone know when and how to use them to greatest effect.

If you want to master Shakespeare, you must rise above that prejudice of our age and take a big step into the true delights of Elizabethan Rhetoric. I'm not suggesting that you need to learn the Latin names of two hundred Rhetorical Figures. But you do need to know when your character is using a formal figure and why and what the point is.

The thing is, people and characters use figures of speech to heighten impact, to clarify, to persuade, to impress. You know perfectly well that it is your brilliant playwright who uses these figures so effectively. Because your character knows why he or she uses them, **you** must find an understanding of why your character does it.

What is the shape of the figure and how can you illuminate it, fully exploit it? When a formal figure appears, it's not just more talk; it's something special. A figure is like a song; it has its own shape, its own tune, in a sense. Missing this tune is like not noticing that the line your character is saying is a snippet from a pop song and needs the melody to have fullest impact.

ANTITHESIS: SHAKESPEARE'S FAVORITE FIGURE

It isn't possible to develop the whole range of Rhetoric here so I refer you to Sister Miriam Joseph's fine book, *Shakespeare's Use of the Arts of Language* and Bertram Joseph's *Acting Shakespeare*. I want to work with one specific case, a Rhetorical Figure of great power which is too often abused by over-generalizing actors: **Antithesis**.

Shakespeare loved Antithesis and used it constantly. When it appears, it takes charge. That is, it dominates the sentences in which it appears. If you fail to notice that your line contains an Antithesis, or two or three or more, you are in grave danger of turning the line into a counter-melody confusion.

It is one of my life's irritants that I constantly have to point out missed Antitheses and teach the technique of speaking them to actors who use Antithesis in their daily lives almost as often as Shakespeare did in the plays and who never fail to speak them correctly with maximum clarity and emphasis without having to give it a thought. They don't know what they're doing but they sure know how to do it.

Yet they miss Antitheses in the script. And these are not obscure in Shakespeare; they are in plain view and usually undisguised. There is no trick to finding them. If you ever needed proof that many actors are not meaning enough onstage, this is it. Too many are still trapped in the effort to sound good while the countless nuances of meaning which would, in fact, make them sound good go unexplored.

Here are some academic definitions of Antithesis:

> "The juxtaposition of contrasting ideas in balanced phrases";

> "sets contraries in action to give greater perspicuity by contrast";

> ". . . the joining of opposite or contrasting ideas, often in parallel structure."

Antithesis: Shakespeare's Favorite Figure

The two key ideas are *contrast* and *parallelism*.

THE KEY TO PERFORMANCE: When an Antithesis appears in a sentence, it dominates or becomes the focal point of that sentence. Everything in the sentence must work to draw attention to that balanced contrast. Giving the contrasting ideas greatest emphasis is just the beginning.

Mistakes that disperse focus don't happen only to beginners. Recently, on network television, I heard a commercial announcer make this error:

"We don't just ask **questions**. We **answer** them."

I call the contrasting ideas that are the heart of any Antithesis the "**elements**" of the Anti-thesis. The elements of this Antithesis, the contrasting ideas, are "ask" and "answer." By dropping "ask" and punching "questions," the announcer created a diversion that lead to a mental lurch when we got to the second half of the sentence. He defused the punchy little line and masked its point. It happens all the time. I hear it in almost every Shakespearean performance.

Antitheses come in all sizes: 3-element, 4-, 5-, 6-, *et cetera*. The one above had three: *ask/answer* in relation to *questions*.

Find the Antithesis here:

Why should I war without the walls of Troy	TC 1.1.2
That find such cruel battle here within?	TC 1.1.3

I'm sure you spotted *without/within* as the two key elements. ("Without," means "outside" in this case.) More than half of the actors who read this line for me choose "Troy" as the key word in the first line. Something tells them that a preposition can't bear the most important idea. If they don't spot the Antithesis, they'll obscure the meaning of the line that the unfamiliar word had already made difficult. The strongest emphasis in this line should be given to "without" and almost as much to "within."

Here is a six-element example, which is still very simple to spot:

> And let my liver rather heat with wine   MV 1.1.81
> Than my heart cool with mortifying groans.   MV 1.1.82

Try to find the pairs of elements before you read on.
Elements: *liver/heart, heat/cool, wine/groans.*
Easy to spot; perhaps not so easy to speak. Each of the pairs must be made to rise up and make itself noticed. That's a big job.

It can get harder. Here is an eight-element Antithesis made up of four pairs:

> Drown desperate sorrow in dead Edward's grave   R3 2.2.99
> And plant your joys in living Edward's throne.   R3 2.2.100

The pairs are *drown/plant, sorrow/joys, dead/living, grave/throne.*

Some writing, huh? Feel the power of both the contrast and the parallelism.

This gives the actor a lot of work to do. It is essential to make the audience notice each of these comparisons. Clearly it will take a bit of time and quite a bit of emphasis. This couplet is great for practice.

One final demonstration of how astonishingly high Shakespeare's flights of antithetical fancy sometimes took him. Here are the last ten lines of his
Sonnet 129. See how many Antitheses you can find here.
Make it fun; don't peek at my list.

> Enjoyed no sooner but despised straight,
> Past reason hunted, and no sooner had,
> Past reason hated, like a swallow'd bait
> On purpose laid to make the taker mad;
> Mad in pursuit and in possession so,

> Had, having, and in quest to have, extreme;
> A bliss in proof and prove'd, a very woe;
> Before, a joy propos'd; behind, a dream.
> All this the world well knows, yet none knows well
> To shun the heav'n that leads men to this hell.

These are the paired elements I find. Amazing, 12 Antitheses in 10 lines!

> Enjoy'd / despised
> hunted / had
> hunted / hated
> pursuit / possession
> Had / having / in quest to have (a rare 3-part package)
> bliss / woe
> proof / prov'd
> before / behind
> joy proposed / dream
> the world / none
> well knows / knows well
> heav'n / hell

What skill it takes to make all of these contrasts clear and meaningful, given the variety of interwoven images and hard juxtapositions, not to mention a few slightly esoteric words! This sonnet is a great exercise piece. It challenges the actor on many fronts. **Without** specificity of meaning and precise awareness of structure, the whole thing collapses. **With** those things, it is a virtuoso piece. (That, by the way, was an Antithesis spanning two sentences: *without/with*.) The Antithesis is a great entry point into the wealth of Shakespeare's rhetorical world. There is so much of it and study is repaid so quickly and fully that it usually motivates the actor to a more eager study of Elizabethan Rhetoric and every step in that direction enriches Shakespearean performance.

IMAGERY: HOW TO LIVE IN A RICHER WORLD

Everything I just said about Rhetoric applies equally to Imagery. Shakespeare is a master of this non-literal language. His characters, in different ways and to different degrees, are always reaching into the world of metaphor and simile to clarify, vivify, persuade, energize. Characters draw their imagery from worlds which have special meaning for them and by their choices they reveal who they are. Falstaff represents the world of the flesh and the earth and all his imagery comes from this universe. If we want to find the heart of Richard III's mind, we look at his imagery and find he sees himself as gambling at impossible odds, "all the world to nothing." (Wow! Now that is a long shot.) Macbeth, the usurper of a greater man's throne, is given away by images of clothing too large for the wearer and the world of the play is established by a superabundance of darkness, blood, and fearful cries in the night imagery. Shakespeare defines almost every character with individualized image clusters.

> **When characters need to be most eloquent, they go to the worlds they know and love best, or to the worlds which haunt them, for their images. If you want to know them and bring them to life, you must go there too. Speaking the words is not enough. You must imagine them.**

Images are not like normal, literal language. When a character uses a living image, he or she must go to that imagined world to see, hear, smell, feel, in some way experience the imagined; it is that re-experiencing which makes the language of imagery so vivid and special.

> **To speak an image without experiencing it makes it a dead image and that makes your character a flat personality, lacking in imagination. One of the surest ways to make your character big, charismatic, and irresistibly interesting is to connect fully to every possible image and let your inner world become enormous.**

HIS DEVELOPING STYLE

It is very clear that Shakespeare was a constant experimenter with dramatic style. Every time he masters a genre, he moves on. Soon he simply passes beyond the crowd and has to start inventing new genres.

Here are samples of typical verse from four representative moments spanning his career which show the developing complexity of Shakespeare's style (its variety and difficulty) as he matures.

Loves Labour's Lost   1594 LLL 4.3.326 – 330

> From women's eyes this doctrine I derive:
> They sparkle still the right Promethean fire;
> They are the books, the arts, the academes,
> That show, contain, and nourish all the world,
> Else none at all in aught proves excellent.

All five of these lines are standard: 5 iambs, no variations except for two with very minor Caesuras which are only there because the two lists require them; all lines end-stopped. This regularity is typical of the late 16th century. Most other writers stayed with it or moved on to forms so loose they are indistinguishable from prose. Shakespeare played with it a bit, mastered it, and then moved on to more intricate forms.

The regularity gives the verse a strong flavor of artificiality, which was a term of praise in Shakespeare's time and is still a lot of fun **if** it is played accurately, simply, and boldly. The audience will be more consciously aware that it is hearing verse. The actor should face up to this artifice, accept it, and make the most of it. If the actor tries to "naturalize" this verse, it turns out to be very clumsy prose and the thing which gives the play its special sparkle is lost.

2 Henry IV 1598 2H4 2.3.26 – 32

> For those that could speak low and tardily
> Would turn their own perfection to abuse
> To seem like him: so that in speech, in gait,
> In diet, in affections of delight,
> In military rules, humours of blood,
> He was the mark and glass, copy and book,
> That fashioned others.

This represents a large step forward in complexity. The first stop is a Major Caesura in the middle of the third line. The second major idea extends over three full lines and two half-lines. Yet we still have only masculine lines and there are only two inversions, and the four Minor Caesuras are, once again, all just lists.

Antony and Cleopatra 1607 ANT 5.2.87 – 92

> There was no winter in't; an autumn 'twas
> That grew the more by reaping. His delights
> Were dolphin-like; they show'd his back above
> The element they liv'd in; in his liv'ry
> Walked crowns and crownets; realms and islands were
> As plates dripp't from his pocket.

Here we have another major growth in complexity. There are no inversions and only one feminine ending. Shakespeare is playing with the dynamic possibilities of line stops and lilts. All six lines have Major Caesuras. The first line is stopped at the end of the 3rd foot; the third line is stopped after the 2nd foot; lines two, four, and six are stopped in the middle of the 4th foot. None of these lines is end-stopped and so every one requires a lilt. This is a very intricate and purposeful pattern. If you play this pattern fully, you will find that it gives great vigor to the speech. But you will also find that it is a major acting challenge. This is where your skill climbs the hill. I want you to work hard and fast on this advanced level … because I have a much tougher test yet to come.

His Developing Style

The Tempest, 1611 TEM 2.1.250 – 258

> She that is queen of Tunis; she that dwells
> Ten leagues beyond man's life; she that from Naples
> Can have no note, unless the sun were post,
> The man i'th'moon's too slow, till new-born chins
> Be rough and razorable; she that from whom
> We all were sea-swallowed, though some cast again,
> And by that destiny, to perform an act
> Whereof what's past is prologue; what to come
> In yours and my discharge.

By 1611, the year Shakespeare retired, he had learned to complicate his verse extremely without letting it degenerate into prose. This kind of verse, loaded with variations and intricate in its syntax, is both a challenge and an opportunity for an actor. It takes labor to find your way through this line and it requires a great musical skill to perform it so that the audience understands it.

Notice that none of the eight full lines is end-stopped. All lines have a Caesura, 6 Major, 3 Minor. See how deftly he shifts the stop-points around:

> 3.5/ 3/ 2/ 3/ 3/ 2.5/ 2.5/ 3.5/ 3 (.5 = half-foot).

If you prefer words to numbers, the Caesuras come after:

> Tunis, life, note, slow, razorable, swallowed, destiny, prologue and discharge.

All but one line is masculine; six lines require a lilt at line end. Only one is inverted. There are two implied parenthetical units imbedded in the speech. It's amazingly rich.

Shakespeare was playing with stops, lilts, and syntax. You need to feel his game to speak this line very well. It's like an operatic aria, a show piece. And it's more like Stravinsky than Mozart.

As you try to find your way to the meaning of this line, imagine parentheses around "unless the sun . . . too slow" and "though some cast . . . my discharge." You will find that you can make good dramatic sense out of the line but you can't find a completely "proper" grammatical meaning.

Here is a rough paraphrase of what it is saying: "We were drowned and then cast up on the land, presenting us with an opportunity which is obviously our destiny (to kill the king and seize the throne); our lives till now have been preparation for this great act and now it is all up to us. Don't worry about the queen finding out; she is so far away that it will be a done thing long before she hears of it."

I had to rearrange the sequence of ideas and I needed more words than Shakespeare to say what I think he is saying and yet I still only captured a small part of what he says. This is rich stuff and, like all rich dramatic material, it demands great interpretive and expressive work from the actor. Start with an approximation of the meaning, then find the rhythm, then make your meaning so precise, so nuanced, that each word requires its own rhythm, melody, and texture. Then be determined to be understood and believed by the character to whom you are speaking. Do all this and both the clarity and excitement of the speech will emerge.

As you can see, Shakespeare's verse gets much more complex and interesting as he matures in his craft. With his early plays, the verse-speaker's biggest problem is to keep the musical value of the verse without letting the extreme regularity of it become boring. Hang on to the nuances of meaning and they will enliven the strictly iambic lines.

With Shakespeare's late plays, the verse-speaker's biggest challenge is to find the meaning and trace its intricate shape without losing the underlying pulse of the blank verse. Always, the form of the actor's expression has its roots in an awareness of the precise meaning of each moment and the sincere desire to be understood and believed.

> "I pray you, mar no more of my verse with
> Reading them ill-favouredly."
>
> Orlando, As You Like It, 3.2.254-255

MARKING A SCRIPT

In the best of theatrical worlds, every production of Shakespeare would be based on a "performance edition" which was spelled and marked so as to reveal the rhythmic features and pronunciations necessary if what Shakespeare wrote as verse is to be heard as verse. Unfortunately, the only such scripts I know of are the ones I've prepared for my own productions and they aren't yet published.

Until such scripts do appear, we'll be doing our own scansion and when we do, if we're smart we'll mark our findings systematically in our scripts. Here is a simple, clear system for recording the most important rhythmic features.

First, don't mark anything that is "stock." Mark only the variations. If you are working on a line which has one inversion but which is stock in every other way, mark only that inversion. Like this:

    – u /
Ma-ny the time I sat and talked with her.

The slash, in this case, appears only after the foot. That's because this is the first foot. **If any other foot had been inverted, the slash mark would appear both before and after**, like this: / – **u** /.

If this had been a line with a **feminine ending**, you would mark it this way:

    – u /   / u
Many the time we sat and talked toge/ther.

Notice the slash mark placed before the eleventh syllable to indicate feminine ending. Also a good idea to write "fem" in the right margin.

Shakespeare's Verse: A User's Manual

Words ending in "ed": the "ed" may be silent or pronounced. For example, *talked* might be TALK-ehd (as we often say BLESS-ed) or it might be TALKD (as we say *fished* or *wished*). Learn which by scanning your line. Don't rely on your texts. They are inconsistent. The easiest way to indicate the short form is to substitute an apostrophe for the "e": talk'd. You can just leave the **e** there for the longer form.

When a vowel or syllable is **elided** (omitted) replace the vowel with an **apostrophe** ('). Do not pronounce that vowel. Example: HEAV'n is a one-syllable word; RIP'ning (for ripening) is a two-syllable word. More examples: gen'ral = GEN-ruhl; Alb'ny = AHLB-nee. When you speak the shorter forms, do it boldly and crisply; **don't try to "sneak" the elided vowel back in**. Say ROHM-yoh, not ROHM-eyo. Alternately, indicate an elision by striking through the omitted vowel with a slash mark: gen/ral, or omitting the elided vowel and substituting an apostrophe, for example desp'rate.

When a word is shortened not by elision but by compression, by "squeezing," we use this mark ⌢ (called a **"compression mark"**) which indicates that **the sounds within the mark are all spoken as one syllable**. Examples:

many a = two syllables: MEN-yuh; Romeo = two syllables: ROHM-yoh.

Sometimes Shakespeare gives a word **more syllables than we usually give it** or more than it has previously been given in this script. Example: "Romeo" is almost always a two syllable word (ROHM-yoh). Because we are used to giving it three syllables, use the "compression" mark. But on the few occasions when Shakespeare gives it three syllables, put **U** – marks over the last two syllables:

    – u –
    Romeo

If – U marks are preceded and followed by a slash mark (/–U/), they indicate an inversion. If there are no slashes, the line is normal. Why mark a normal foot? To warn of danger in a situation where Modern Quirks might encourage a wrong emphasis. Like this:

         u – u
    That no revenue hast but thy good spirits   HAM 3.2.68

Mark a **Cascade** with an upward slanting line above the syllables of the Cascade from first to last.

> E.g., And the beholders of . . .

The Cascade line would begin low above "And" and rise through "hold."

You will find **lines which are not the usual 5 or 5½ feet**. They may be 2½, 3, or 3½ feet (and we will discuss the purposes of these short lines later) or they may be 6 or 6½ feet. In these cases, write the length of the line in the right margin. (6½ ft., for example) And then get busy figuring out **why** the length is odd. The most common cause of the 6 ½-foot line is the Silent Beat in mid-line. Here's a sample:

> Murder'd her kinsman. **X** O, tell me friar, tell me   ROM 3.3.105

In my experience, most actors and directors find it too easy to forget the Lilts and they fail to notice the harm this does to the meaning and mood. Every verse line that **doesn't** end with a stop (that is, with the end of a thought, a . ; : ? or !) needs a Lilt of some useful shape. To jog your memory, put a mark at the end of every Liltable line. See p. 45 for more on the Lilt.

> And if I fail not in my deep intent   R3 1.1.149

Occasionally, your lines will be **Prose**. When this is the case, you might write "PROSE" in the right margin.

Rarely you will find a verse line that you can't scan according to the system, no matter how carefully you check pronunciation or emphasis or elision or compression possibilities. In these cases, just write "IRR" for "irregular" in the right margin. (The likely explanation of these "irregular" lines is that they were "corrupted in transmission," i.e., errors were made in typesetting or printing. Or perhaps later editors decided that they were verse lines when Shakespeare actually meant them as prose. We'll never know for sure.)

Shakespeare's Verse: A User's Manual

> ACTORS:
> YOUR MISSION,
> SHOULD YOU CHOOSE TO ACCEPT IT,
> is to fit each of your lines to the patterns described above. If you find any that don't fit or which require you to speak in a way which doesn't seem to "work," point those lines out to your director or speech coach. There is a way that works for you and Shakespeare.

CRUCIAL ORGANIC STRATEGY

Don't confuse "discovering the necessary rhythm" with choosing the way of saying the line. When you have found the rhythmic requirements of the line, many nuances of emphasis and melody remain to be discovered and these refinements of expression should grow out of your character and the immediate situation.

Shakespeare's verse rhythms can give you a powerful foundation for your performance.

They will help you in many ways without inhibiting your creativity or individuality. A little bit of thoughtful work at the beginning of the rehearsal process will keep you from being just one more actor who speaks Shakespeare's wonderful verse plays as if they were written in prose.

TESTIMONY FROM THE SKILLED AND FAMOUS:

"You come back to Shakespeare with such relief, such joy. He's done all the work for you. All you have to do is breathe it in and speak it out; just let it live in the air. This is, of course, easier said than done. But only by doing it, by practicing the skills, will you eventually learn to master them."

Anthony Sher, a star classical actor in England

SPEECHES FOR SCANNING PRACTICE WITH MY SOLUTIONS

Try scanning these speeches,

then flip to the next page for my version.

Mark only variations and warnings.

This is Duke Senior in *AYL* 2.1.2

> Hath not old custom made this life more sweet
>
> Than that of painted pomp? Are not these woods
>
> More free from peril than the envious court?
>
> Now, my co-mates and brothers in exile,
>
> Here feel we but the penalty of Adam,
>
> The seasons' difference, as the icy fang
>
> And churlish chiding of the winter's wind,
>
> Which, when it bites and blows upon my body,
>
> Even till I shrink with cold, I smile and say
>
> "This is no flattery: these are counsellors
>
> That feelingly persuade me what I am."
>
> Sweet are the uses of adversity,
>
> Which, like the toad, ugly and venomous,
>
> Wears yet a precious jewel in his head;
>
> And this our life exempt from public haunt
>
> Finds tongues in trees, books in the running brooks,
>
> Sermons in stones and good in every thing.
>
> I would not change it.

Speeches for Scanning Practice

Remember that when we use the lighter/heavier marks *without* slash marks before and after, they are meant to indicate that the rhythm is normal but you might be tempted by Modern Speech Quirks to emphasize the wrong syllable here. Look for places where I have removed letters and replaced them with apostrophes.

Hath not old custom made this life more sweet

Than that of painted pomp? Are not these woods

More free from peril than the en͡vious court?

    u –   **u –**
Now, my co-mates and brothers in exile,

Here feel we but the penalty of Ad/am,

The seasons' diff'rence, as the icy fang

And churlish chiding of the winter's wind,

Which, when it bites and blows upon my bo/dy

E͡en till I shrink with cold, I smile and say

"This is no flatt'ry: these are counsellors

That feelingly persuade me what I am."

Sweet are the uses of adversity,   [1ˢᵗ foot = judgment call]

     / – u /
Which, like the toad, ugly and venomous,

     – u
Wears yet a precious jewel in his head;

And this our life exempt from public haunt

     / – **u/**
Finds tongues in trees, books in the running brooks,

 – u /   **– u –**
Sermons in stones and good in every thing.

I would not change it.

Here is a speech from *Cymbeline*, 1.1.28, spoken by The First Gentleman. The scansion will tell you how to pronounce the unfamiliar names. Put emphasis marks on all of the names.

I cannot delve him to the root: his father

Was call'd Sicilius, who did join his honour

Against the Romans with Cassibelan,

But had his titles by Tenantius whom

He served with glory and admir'd success,

So gain'd the sur-addition Leonatus;

And had, besides this gentleman in question,

Two other sons, who in the wars o' th' time

Died with their swords in hand; for which their father . . .

Speeches for Scanning Practice

Compare your scan with mine.

    I cannot delve him to the root: his fa/ther

             u – u
    Was call'd Sicilius, who did join his honor

                      u – u –
    Against the Romans with Cassibelan,

                 u – u
    But had his titles by Tenantius whom

    He served with glory and admir'd success,

                 – u – u
    So gain'd the sur-addition Leona/tus;

    And had, besides this gentleman in question,

    Two other sons, who in the wars o' th time

    –   u /
    Died with their swords in hand; for which their fa/ther . . .

This one is from *Coriolanus*, 1.1.165, and the speaker is the title character himself. Having just won the war for Rome, he is very angry to see the citizens protesting in the streets. He is easily angered.

> He that will give good words to thee will flatter
>
> Beneath abhorring. What would you have, you curs,
>
> That like nor peace nor war? the one affrights you,
>
> The other makes you proud. He that trusts to you,
>
> Where he should find you lions, finds you hares;
>
> Where foxes, geese: you are no surer, no,
>
> Than is the coal of fire upon the ice,
>
> Or hailstone in the sun. Your virtue is
>
> To make him worthy whose offence subdues him
>
> And curse that justice did it. Who deserves great-ness
>
> Deserves your hate; and your affections are
>
> A sick man's appetite, who desires most that
>
> Which would increase his evil. He that depends
>
> Upon your favors swims with fins of lead
>
> And hews down oaks with rushes. Hang ye! Trust Ye?

Speeches for Scanning Practice

Here is my version.

    He that will give good words to thee will flat/ter

    Beneath abhorring. **X** What would you have, you curs,   (6ft.)

    That like nor peace nor war? the one affrights/ you,

    The other makes you proud. **X** He that trusts to you,   (6 ft.)

    Where he should find you lions, finds you hares;

    Where foxes, geese: you are no surer, no,

    Than is the coal of fire upon the ice, (**fi** – ruh – **PON**)

    Or hailstone in the sun. Your virtue is

    To make him worthy whose offence subdues/ him

                               / – u / u - / u
    And curse that justice did it. **X** Who deserves great-ness

    Deserves your hate; and your affections are

                                 / u   –
    A sick man's app'tite, who desires most that

    Which would increase his evil. **X** He that depends (or 1-syll "evil")

    Upon your favors swims with fins of lead

    And hews down oaks with rushes. Hang ye! Trust Ye?

Sonnet 30 is much abused. See if you can find its sweet shape:

    When to the sessions of sweet silent thought

    I summon up remembrance of things past,

    I sigh the lack of many a thing I sought,

    And with old woes new wail my dear time's waste:

    Then can I drown an eye, unused to flow,

    For precious friends hid in death's dateless night,

    And weep afresh love's long since cancell'd woe,

    And moan the expense of many a vanish'd sight:

    Then can I grieve at grievances foregone,

    And heavily from woe to woe tell o'er

    The sad account of fore-bemoaned moan,

    Which I new pay as if not paid before.

        But if the while I think on thee, dear friend,

        All losses are restored and sorrows end.

Speeches for Scanning Practice

Here is my take on it. Most actors get caught in a dactylic rhythm at the start which clashes with the smooth rhythm Shakespeare chose to suggest his sweet silent sessions.

When to the sessions of sweet silent thought

I summon up remembrance of things past,

I sigh the lack of many a thing I sought,

And with old woes new wail my dear time's waste:

   –   u /
Then can I drown an eye, unused to flow,

           / –   u /
For precious friends hid in death's dateless night,

And weep afresh love's long since cancell'd woe,

And moan the expense of many a vanish'd sight:

   –   u /
Then can I grieve at grievances foregone,

And heavily from woe to woe tell o'er

The sad account of fore-bemoaned moan,

Which I new pay as if not paid before.

      But if the while I think on thee, dear friend,

      All losses are restor'd and sorrows end.

APPENDIX 1: END OF THE BEGINNING. SO NOW WHAT?

There you have an introduction to the greatness of the best playwright of all time and maker of the meatiest acting-stuff ever.

Shakespeare's greatness, I believe lies in the inconceivable range and depth of his understanding of our humanity. He seems to have seen us all, clearly, profoundly, and without prejudice and he gave each of us a full chance to express ourselves. Unlike almost every other writer, he didn't stack the deck.

Put that incredible insight together with his rare open mind and all you need to complete the greatest writer ever is total mastery of the medium. His gift of language defies comprehension. Only a few others in history have matched his vocabulary of over 26,000 words. We are told he invented an average of eighty-one new words per script. Shakespeare found such cut-to-the-heart ways of expressing our thoughts and feelings that his way of saying things has, to an amazing degree, become our way of saying those things.

There's an old joke that carries a lot of truth with it: The traditional little old lady sees a production of *Hamlet*. At the end, she turns to her lady friend and says, "I don't see what's so wonderful about that. It's just a long string of clichés." And it's true. We love his words so much we repeat them into clichédom.

I hope that at this point you have the fundamental information you need to scan most blank verse lines accurately.

I hope, too, that you understand the problem of pronunciation shift that stands in the way of good scansion, even when we understand the basic system.

It is very important that you remember to work out your scansion at the very beginning of your process, not after you have started to lock in your readings and your Subtext.

Let's assume that you are serious about performing or directing or teaching, or even reading Shakespeare. It follows then that you have taken the pains to understand and to apply the fundamentals of his verse system which you found in this book. You get the idea.

When asked, you can scan a line. On stage, you can work out the rhythm of your lines and, if encouraged, will give a true verse performance, which makes people wonder why you seem so much clearer and more interesting than most of the others on the stage with you.

Good. You've taken step one.

If you're a director, you've probably reached the point where you can scan a line yourself and help the needy actor who's smart enough to come to you.

If you've really applied yourself, you have not only conquered the impulse to say "Ro-me-o and Ju-li-et" but you flinch appropriately when you hear others say it.

Now what?

Take step two: drill your verse speaking skills until the sound and feel of the rhythm becomes so familiar, so natural, that you instantly recognize any variation from it. Till you become a self-correcting actor. Till you feel the rightness of his rhythm and its organic connection to his thought and feeling so fully that an error in rhythm is felt as a failure of the foundation of your dramatic structure, a speed bump on your highway, a wrong note in your symphony.

If you are a director, you will be ready for Shakespeare when you can hear the correctness of every actor's rhythm and every deviation from it. When you have this, you have your foundation. Then you are ready to go forth and build great palaces.

And then you are ready to take up another responsibility . . . to go forth and multiply. Share what you have learned here with the poor, prose-speaking actors of the world.

APPENDIX 2: HOW I DID MY RESEARCH AND WHY I DIDN'T PUT THAT IN THE BOOK

I began this book by telling you how I learned that more was needed in performing Shakespeare's verse than I had ever dreamed. I describe my disappointment when I found there was very little in print about the performing of Shakespeare's verse, and my determination to do whatever it took to fill this gap in my and our educations. Forty years of work went into the project before I felt fully prepared to write the book I needed but couldn't find. Six versions of the book, under the name *The Shak-Pack*, were written before I found satisfaction. By this time I felt extremely apostolic about . . . what is it? Protecting directors and actors? Or protecting Shakespeare?

It didn't take more than a couple of years to find out there was almost nothing substantial in the field. Yes, there are a few good books about vocal technique, but even the best voice and speech teachers didn't understand the rhythmic factor called verse. There were several examples of high scholarship which had almost no pragmatic value for performers or readers.

So I committed to do serious research, whatever was necessary, until I could feel like an honorable man when telling people: "No, that's not it. This is it." I walked a long path in which there was searching, frustration, excitement, confusion, disappointment, and finally, jubilation!

This is the order in which I did my research.

- Examined modern work on comprehending and performing Shakespeare's verse. Strike out.
- Examined critical works by 15th, 16th and 17th century writers. *Abbondanza!*
- Scanned works that are written in iambic pentameter.
- Scanned Shakespeare's verse. First word by word; that is, all the appearances of word "a," all the appearances of word "b," all the appearances of word . . . . Then, I scanned Shakespeare's plays chronologically, that is, from scene 1 to the last scene. This is the mother lode. Without it, there's no game.

Appendix 2: How I Did My Research and Why I Didn't Put That in the Book

- Searched for the evidence of how iambic pentameter stopped being a standard. Interesting but not crucial.
- Examined what happened to verse speech as a result. The correct speaking of iambic pentameter stopped being a standard.
- Examined the earliest works on English Poesy. Again, fun, but less productive than the Elizabethan stuff.
- Tested the understandings I had developed in production to see if they really mattered, to see what the best way of leading actors down the iambic pentameter path was.
- Studied audience responses to my shows and found them to be positive. Example: It is typical for audiences at Shakespeare plays to complain that the play was slow at the beginning. Since I've been able to train actors in verse speaking, I have never heard that complaint. It turns out that the problem was not the tempo of the words but rather, the tempo of information flow. The more information gets passed, the faster the show feels, although it may actually be slower. The verse enhances clarity.
- Listened to verse in a wide variety of contexts. Ongoing. Valuable and essential.
- Began writing and testing the book as a user's manual. Most of this happened in classes I taught and Shakespeare performances I directed.
- Scholarly exchange. Ongoing. You are welcome to join the fun.
- Continue to observe many productions of Shakespeare, always listening and asking where the errors in rhythm are and how they might be fixed.

Scholarly writing is seldom read in our time. I want this book, above all, to be a practical handbook, and so I have eliminated everything possible which might discourage, bore, or otherwise turn away readers. If I did full scale scholarly citations, for example, there would be so many they might outweigh the content of the book. I'm aware that this may turn away serious scholars. I hope not. But it is a risk that must be undertaken if this book is to be as used and useful as it is meant to be.

APPENDIX 3: WHAT ABOUT / UU / AND / -- / WHY NO / -UU / ? WHY NO / UU- / ?

You may know enough about metrics to recognize / UU / and / -- / as kinds of verse foot which I didn't deal with in the main text. Now that I'm confessing, I might as well slip in two other verse forms that I chose to ignore.

Dactylic: / — u u /

Anapaest: (antidactylus) / u u — /

Let us dispose of the 3-syllable dactyl and the anapaest. People who haven't looked deeply enough into the pronunciation shifts since Shakespeare's time or into Shakespeare's deep commitment to the iambic form often try to work their way out of scansion problems by adding that 3rd syllable to the foot. One little misguided dactyl can throw a whole line off.

Shakespeare's commitment to the iambic foot is profound and his commitment to the 10 or 11 syllable line is even more intense. **He is deeply committed to these forms.**

The iamb is the only foot Shakespeare mentions and the "tenner" is his nickname for the length of the line. Thomas Nashe identifies the line with the label "drumming decasyllabons." "Deca" for "ten" and "syllabons" for "syllables." "Drumming" suggests the regularity, the consistency of the iambic pentameter. The Elizabethan playwrights generally used "numbers" as a nickname for verse.

If you think carefully about this issue of feet with more than two syllables you'll see that "3-syllable" substitutions are not only disruptive, they also complicate rather than simplify the job of reconciling the lines.

As you come to understand the flexibility of the iambic foot and its deep roots in our heartbeat you'll want to hang on to the iamb. You won't need the dactyls and anapests.

Appendix 3: What About / UU / and / -- /? Why No / –uu /? Why No / --U /

You won't need any non-iambic feet except, of course, for the trochee, which, as you'll remember we call an Inversion.

The pyrrhus and spondee signs tell us that the 2 syllables are of equal emphasis.

The pyrrhus / uu / represents two of what they call (but I don't) two "light" emphases and the spondee / -- / represents two "heavy" syllables. I challenge you to make an audience hear that distinction. A phenomenon that has tantalized me since I first realized it, is that in performance, the context of an iambic play, two technically equal syllables will sound iambic. That is one reason to forget about two equal syllables.

Anyway, playwrights shouldn't try to micro-manage the vocal shape of the play to that degree. By the time we get to such refinements, we can't trust anything but character and Subtext to determine the amount of emphasis. Once you've found a fundamental iambic pattern, let your understanding of the purposes of the line determine the subtleties of emphasis.

In our system, relativity is at the heart of the matter.

APPENDIX 4: HOW TO GET HELP PRONOUNCING SHAKESPEARE'S WORDS

It's not always as easy as I wish to determine the proper pronunciation of a word. Rigorous scansion is the most reliable approach and careful use of a good concordance such as Spewack's or David and Ben Crystals'. Recently published manuscript versions of the earliest attempts at dictionaries in Shakespeare's time will help us immensely with our pronunciation problems.

Two of the most useful aids in this job are the reforming orthographers of Shakespeare's time. A reforming orthographer is a scholar who wants to make our language clear and consistent, and to do that, tries to make the words look like they sound.

My two favorites are: William Bullokar and John Hart. These guys are reforming orthographers of Shakespeare's period. Here are some examples from William Bullokar, of what a consistent language might look like. It is not too hard to count the syllables here. We may trust their spelling to reveal much about their pronunciation. Of course they don't spell the whole of the language for us. But we can learn much from the samples they provided. Above all, we learn about similarities among words and we get strong evidence for a key fact: many words were spoken in much briefer form than we now use. For example, in every use, Bullokar spells "heaven" and "reason" without the final vowel. This fits with the spelling found in Shakespeare and leads us to the conclusion that both words were in general usage and for Shakespeare, both were monosyllables. John Hart, trying to devise spelling which reveals pronunciations, gives us these single-spacing spellings: "heavn" and "reasn."

Two of the hardest words to define without the help of the orthographer: "heavn" and "reasn," usually spoken as two 1-syllable words, are his version of "heaven" and "reason."

This spelling together with other powerful evidence, makes it easy to buy the idea that "heaven" is a one syllable word most of the time.

Above all, these orthographers teach us much with their samples. The John Hart samples, here, are in the left column, followed by the orthographer's recommended clarification on the right.

the image	=	thimage
the experience	=	thexperience
the objections	=	thobjections
the other	=	thother
the accidents	=	thaccidents
learned	=	learnd
I would	=	ei – uld
Heaven	=	Hevn

Hart's "Hevn" is a bit easier to buy than Bullokar's "heavn," but they both want the same thing: heaven without the closing "e."

This kind of scholarly work is what taught us to say:
"there**for**," "where**for**" and "there**by**," which we had traditionally spoken with first syllable emphasis, and which Hart taught us to give last syllable emphasis.

MUSIC

Music is one of the strongest sources of evidence for pronunciation. Shakespeare's England left us a huge treasure trove of songs. As you know, most of the time, words match music in songs and you can tell a lot about the length and emphasis requirements of the lyrics. You look at the notes and they tell you what's long and what's short. The notation tells you how many syllables.

Now, despite their value, you don't need to be doing an analysis of orthographers work or music, and you don't need to be carrying your concordance around in your backpack. These aren't techniques you need to use all the time, except for scansion. But when you need solid evidence to get answers, they can be extremely useful. I used all of them and it was of tremendous value.

APPENDIX 5: THE CONVERSATION

Over the years, teaching this material to eager learners at all levels, I have had to face one thing: no matter how carefully I describe the material, it doesn't become really clear until I demonstrate it. It's easy to say "flow, don't chop" but what does that really sound like? Same for those pesky Didleys and Cascades and Lilts.

I've tried to clarify several of these possibly vague or ambiguous matters in an online supplement which is housed on the book's website. I suggest that you read the book and come to your own understandings before diving into my demos and coaching, which you will find online at the book's website:

www.ShakespearesVerse-UsersManual.com

Feel free to post your questions or arguments at my website.
I look forward to our conversation.

ONE LAST EXHORTATION, DIRECT FROM WILLIAM S.

> The man that hath no music in himself,
>
> Nor is not moved with concord of sweet sounds,
>
> Is fit for treasons, stratagems, and spoils.
>
> The motions of his spirit are dull as night,
>
> And his affections dark as Erebus.
>
> Let no such man be trusted.
>
> MV, 5.1.83-88

The verse rhythm is the necessary foundation of Shakespeare's potent music.

Get that rhythm section going.

Joy of the Bard to you,

Roger Gross

Made in the USA
Middletown, DE
12 January 2018